Not-for-Profit
Audit Committee
Best Practices

NOT-FOR-PROFIT AUDIT COMMITTEE BEST PRACTICES

WARREN RUPPEL, C.P.A.

WILEY

John Wiley & Sons, Inc.

For general information on our other products and services, or technical support, please
contact our Customer Care Department within the United States at 800-762-2974,
outside the United States at 317-572-3993 or fax 317-572-4002.

Wiley also publishes its books in a variety of electronic formats. Some content that
appears in print may not be available in electronic books.

For more information about Wiley products, visit our Web site at http://*www.wiley.com*.

Library of Congress Cataloging-in-Publication Data:

ISBN-13 978-0-471-69741-1
ISBN-10 0-471-69741-9

Printed in the United States of America

10 9 8 7 6 5 4 3 2 1

About the Author

Warren Ruppel, CPA, has over 25 years of expertise in governmental and not-for-profit accounting. He is the Director of Government Services at Marks Paneth & Shron, CPAs, New York, where he also serves as part of the firm's quality assurance function. He formerly was the Assistant Comptroller for Accounting of the City of New York, where he was responsible for all aspects of the City's accounting and financial reporting for over 12 years. He was also the Secretary of the City's Audit Committee. He began his career at KPMG, after graduating from St. John's University, New York. He later joined Deloitte & Touche, to specialize in audits of not-for-profit organizations and governments. Mr. Ruppel has also served as the chief financial officer of an international not-for-profit organization and as a partner in a small CPA practice.

Mr. Ruppel has served as instructor for many training courses, including specialized governmental and not-for-profit programs and seminars. He has also been an adjunct lecturer of accounting at the Bernard M. Baruch College of the City University of New York. He is the author of several other books, *OMB Circular A-133 Audits, Not-for-Profit Organization Audits,* and, also published by John Wiley & Sons, Inc., *GAAP for Governments, Governmental Accounting Made Easy* and *Not-for-Profit Accounting Made Easy.*

Mr. Ruppel is a member of the American Institute of Certified Public Accountants, as well as the New York State Society of Certified Public Accountants, where he is chair of the Audit Committee and serves on the Governmental Accounting and Auditing and Not-for-Profit Organizations Technical Committees. He is also a past president of the New York chapter of the Institute of Management Accountants. Mr. Ruppel is a member of the Government Finance Officers Association and serves on its Special Review Committee.

Contents

Preface

Audit committees of not-for-profit organizations play an important role in supporting the financial reporting integrity of these organizations. Numerous recent accounting scandals and financial statement restatements along with drastic changes in the regulatory and standards setting environment have made the work of audit committees far more important, but also far more confusing. While numerous requirements have been legislated for audit committees of public companies, primarily through the Sarbanes-Oxley Act, there is no equivalent set of rules for audit committees of not-for-profit organizations. Which of the Sarbanes-Oxley requirements (if any) should a not-for-profit audit committee adopt? *Not-for-Profit Audit Committee Best Practices* seeks to cut through the current state of confusion and provide a straightforward, hands-on approach for audit committees of not-for-profit organizations to operate in a manner that employs best practices that will best serve their particular organizations.

Chapter 1 presents an overview of the not-for-profit organization operating environment as well as an overview of the financial reporting function of these organizations. Chapter 2 assists in establishing an audit committee, defining its operating principles and establishing a charter. Chapter 3 covers what an audit committee member needs to know about internal control. Chapter 4 discusses fraud in the financial reporting environment. Chapter 5 looks at the best uses of an internal audit function. Chapter 6 describes how an effective whistleblower program can be established. Chapter 7 describes the audit committee's relationship with the organization's independent auditor. Finally, Chapter 8 helps an audit committee establish a committee action plan.

No one set of practices and procedures can be universally applied to all not-for-profit organization audit committees with the designation of being "best practices." Rather, audit committees must be able to evaluate the various options that they have in determining how they operate. This means understanding why a particular practice is or is not important to a particular organization. *Not-for-Profit Audit Committee Best Practices* helps audit committees make these choices by providing a sound knowledge base for decision making as well as providing insights as to how to choose from among practice alternatives.

My thanks go to all those at John Wiley & Sons, Inc. who have enabled this book to become a reality, particularly John DeRemigis, Judy Howarth, and Kerstin Nasdeo. I'm also thankful for my supportive family—my wife Marie and sons Christopher and Gregory.

WARREN RUPPEL
New York, New York
September 2005

Chapter 1

Background and Regulatory Issues

The purpose of this chapter is to set the stage for understanding the various considerations to make when establishing best practices for a not-for-profit organization's audit committee. In other words, to determine those characteristics of these organizations that make them so distinctive that simply mimicking the requirements of audit committees established by other types of organizations (such as the Sarbanes-Oxley Act of 2002, which applies to publicly traded companies) would fail to result in what could be considered best practices for a not-for-profit organization's audit committee.

Specifically, this chapter will address the following:

- The types of not-for-profit organizations covered by this book
- The unique characteristics of not-for-profit organizations
- The financial reporting environment for not-for-profit organizations
- Users of not-for-profit organization financial statements
- The regulatory environment for not-for-profit organizations

Understanding these basics will lay the framework for establishing best practices for whatever type of organization the reader is involved with.

TYPES OF NOT-FOR-PROFIT ORGANIZATIONS COVERED BY THIS BOOK

The term "not-for-profit" encompasses a very broad range of organizations. Major colleges and universities, private schools, as well as hospitals and medical centers are typically organized as not-for-profit organizations. Social service organizations, such as homeless shelters, day care centers, senior citizen centers, are also likely to be set up as not-for-profit organizations. Most religious organizations, too, are established as not-for-profits. In addition, there is a broad range of very small organizations structured at a local level, such as parent-teacher associations, youth sports (soccer, baseball, etc.) groups, to name a few, that are not-for-profit in nature. And let us not leave out political, trade, and professional organizations, and country clubs. From this simple, far from inclusive list, you can see that the needs of a particular organization as to an audit committee will vary greatly. The ideas presented throughout this book will attempt to strike a middle ground—that is, a midsized not-for-profit organization. Where appropriate, ideas for reducing or strengthening the role of an audit committee will be presented so that small and larger organizations can customize the suggestions for their particular circumstances.

UNIQUE CHARACTERISTICS OF NOT-FOR-PROFIT ORGANIZATIONS

What makes not-for-profit organizations so special that they need their own best practices for their audit committees? The easy answer is that not-for-profit organizations do not have as their primary motive the objective to make a profit. But this answer does not explain what makes not-for-profit organizations unique, particularly from a financial accounting and reporting perspective, so let's look at this in a little more depth.

Fortunately, the Financial Accounting Standards Board (FASB), which establishes generally accepted accounting principles (GAAP) for not-for-profit organizations, has already examined this question and presented its "concepts" in its FASB's Concepts Statement No. 4 ("Objectives of Financial Reporting by Nonbusiness Organizations"). Although this concepts statement is fairly old (it was issued in 1980), it was later used by the FASB to formulate the accounting and financial reporting requirements used by not-for-profit organizations today. Therefore, audit committee members would be well advised to gain at least a general understanding of the concepts presented in this document so that they can better work with the foundation of the financial reports issued by not-for-profit organizations.

PERSPECTIVE:

You may be familiar with the debate over whether accounting standards should be more "principles-based" or "rules-based." In other words, should accounting standards present accounting objectives and the basic principles required to be used by an organization in its financial reporting, or should accounting standards present detailed, specific rules for how specific types of transactions are accounted? Recent publicized accounting failures demonstrate that some organizations may have been clever enough to "get around" specific rules, yet technically comply with GAAP, while probably violating the principle (or spirit) on which those particular rules are based. Having a basic understanding of the conceptual framework of financial reporting for not-for-profit organizations can help audit committee members ask the right questions, to ensure that their organization is complying with both the rule and the spirit of any particular accounting standard.

The Concepts Statement No. 4 (Con-4) highlights the following differences between business and nonbusiness enterprises:

> Receipts of significant amounts of resources from resource providers who do not expect to receive either repayment or economic benefits proportionate to resources provided.

A donor that makes a contribution to a not-for-profit organization does not expect a direct benefit of a similar economic amount from the organization as a result of the contribution. Sometimes these types of transactions are called *nonexchange transactions* because the contribution is not exchanged for something; rather, it is given without the expectation that something will be received in return. Contrast this to a business-type transaction where you pay a specific price for some item or service. You are not interested in paying more than the amount of the economic benefit that you receive in return. For example, you pay for the gasoline received when you fill up your car. Many not-for-profit organizations engage in both nonexchange and exchange transactions. A good example would be a not-for-profit school. Tuition is paid for the right to attend the school— an exchange transaction. At the same time, students, parents, and alumni are solicited for contributions to the school. These contributions would be nonexchange transactions.

Some transactions have characteristics of both exchange and nonexchange transactions. For example, assume the aforementioned school holds a bake sale to fund new books for its library. Yes, you would get a cake for your contribution, but you probably wouldn't have bought that cake for the same amount at the local bakery. The transaction is partially an exchange transaction and partially a nonexchange transaction.

> Operating purposes that are other than to provide goods or services at a profit or profit equivalent.

This should be fairly obvious from the name "not-for-profit organization," but it deserves comment to help establish the financial reporting framework that is necessary to understand. A different way to look at this concept is to recognize that a not-for-profit organization's goal is not always to maximize revenues and to minimize expenses, resulting in the greatest amount of excess revenues over expenses. On the revenue side, a not-for-profit organization may not always charge its "customers" the highest that it can for the services it provides. Often, providing services at below a market rate may be the objective of the not-for-profit organization. On the expense side, a distinction needs to be made between an organization's administrative costs and its program costs. While it's true that not-for-profit organizations generally try to minimize their administrative expenses, this is not usually the case with program expenses. Program expenses are those spent on supporting the activities of the not-for-profit organization's reason for being. Most not-for-profit organization try to spend as much on programs as they possibly can without jeopardizing their financial well-being.

On balance, a typical not-for-profit prefers to report in its financial statements a balance between its revenues and expenses, resulting in a small excess or deficiency of revenues over expenses. When a not-for-profit organization's revenues consistently exceed its expenses, it becomes difficult to make the case to donors that their contributions are necessary, since it appears that the organization has more money coming in than it is spending. On the other hand, consistently overspending the revenues that come in can lead a not-for-profit organization to a precarious, or worse, financial condition.

Many additional factors may influence a not-for-profit organization's financial operating practices. For example, a not-for-profit organization may try to have surplus revenues in the short run because it is trying to accumulate resources for some significant program or construction activity that it anticipates in the future. It is important that audit committee members understand these considerations when reading and reviewing the not-for-profit organization's financial statements.

> Absence of defined ownership interests that can be sold, transferred, or redeemed, or that convey entitlement to a share of a residual distribution of resources in the event of liquidation of the organization.

Not-for-profit organizations are created by organizers that come to own no stock or other ownership interest in the organization. These organizations are set up according to various state not-for-profit corporation laws, and obtain tax-exempt status after application to the Internal Revenue Service. The organization has to be set up for purposes of pursuing what it defines as its objective, or *exempt function*, that is appropriate and allowable for a not-for-profit organization. The organization cannot be created for purposes of providing a private financial benefit to the organizers of the organization, successor governing board members, or management members outside of their normal compensation. In other words, a not-for-profit that has accumulated significant net assets by consistently having excesses of revenues over expenses can't be sold or transferred to someone else, nor can the board, management, or the original organizers share in these accumulated resources for their own benefit. Not-for-profit organization audit committee members should be aware of these requirements because they are so different from those of business enterprises. This concept will be reinforced later in this book when we cover conflicts-of-interest statements, which will be recommended to be completed by audit committee members.

FINANCIAL REPORTING ENVIRONMENT OF NOT-FOR-PROFIT ORGANIZATIONS

This section is not intended to present a comprehensive guide to not-for-profit GAAP and financial statement preparation. A number of other resources devoted to specific not-for-profit accounting and financial reporting issues are available to audit committee members. (I have written one such resource, titled *Not-for-Profit Accounting Made Easy*, also published by John Wiley & Sons, Inc. [2002], which an audit committee member will find useful.) Rather, this section describes what an audit committee member should know, and be thinking about, when reading a set of not-for-profit organization's financial statements. As such, let's consider the following important topics regarding the financial reporting environment of not-for-profit organizations.

Basic Financial Statements

As noted earlier, the accounting and financial reporting rules known as GAAP for not-for-profit organizations are established by the FASB. The American Institute of Certified Public Accountants (AICPA) also publishes statements of position, accounting and audit guides, staff position papers, and other resources that, while not as authoritative as FASB statements, contribute to the body of knowledge that constitutes GAAP for not-for-profit organizations. Much of the audit committee's function that is discussed in this book involves ensuring that these basic financial statements are presented fairly in accordance with GAAP. The basic financial statements for not-for-profit organizations comprise the following elements.

Statement of Financial Position.   Many nonaccountants would probably refer to the statement of financial position as a balance sheet. This statement provides a snapshot of a not-for-profit organization's assets, liabilities, and net assets. Net assets represent the difference between total assets and total liabilities. The statement of financial position is prepared as of the not-for-profit organization's fiscal year-end.

Statement of Activities.   The statement of activities presents the increases and decreases to a not-for-profit organization's net assets over a period of time, which for annual financial statements, is for the period representing the entire fiscal year. This statement basically represents the not-for-profit organization's operating or income statements, displaying items that both increased net assets (such as contribution revenues) and decreased net assets (such as resources spent on program or administrative activities.)

Statement of Cash Flows.   The statement of cash flows provides information about the not-for-profit organization's receipts and disbursements of cash. Cash receipts and disbursements in the cash flow statement are classified into three categories: operating activities, investing activities, and financing activities.

Notes to the Financial Statements.   Many readers of the financial statements of not-for-profit organizations overlook the importance of the notes that are part of those statements. The notes are not simply an add-on to the basic financial statements; they are an integral part of the financial statements. The sources for the requirements of the notes to the financial statements are many. Each new FASB statement or pronouncement that is issued, more often than not, includes some new disclosure requirements that must be contained in the notes to the financial statements to address some specific aspect of the new statement or pronouncement.

In addition to the notes required by new statements or pronouncements, there are some core notes that must be included. One of the most significant notes, which is generally the first one reported, is the summary of significant accounting policies. In certain circumstances, not-for-profit organizations can choose among a number of acceptable accounting principles to use. Where such choice exists, the summary of significant accounting policies helps to understand which policies were chosen. This is an important note for audit committee members to read and comprehend. The audit committee should be aware of the selection of accounting policies by the not-for-profit organization and be satisfied that appropriate selections are being made. Sometimes organizations, including not-for-profits, select accounting policies because they serve some particular need or desire of management, rather than strictly on the merits of the various alternatives. While this may be fine for each individual accounting policy selected, the cumulative effect of accounting policy elections may indicate that the financial reporting practices of the organization are aggressive or conservative. Audit committee members should try to get a sense for how and why accounting policies are selected and be comfortable with them individually and collectively.

The Annual Report

Many midsize to large not-for-profit organizations issue an annual report, which is often called a glossy annual report that includes the basic financial statements and other information. The term "glossy" refers to the coated, shiny paper on which the annual report is printed. In addition to the basic financial statements, the annual report usually contains pictures of the organization's programs in action, a letter from the president or executive director, descriptions of program activities, and information about major donors. Because the annual report contains the basic financial statements, audit committee members should review the document to familiarize themselves with its contents and to serve as a control—that is, to ensure that the information presented does not conflict with anything in the basic financial statements. For example, if the executive director's letter in the annual report states that contributions increased 20 percent from the prior fiscal year, but the financial statements report a decrease in contributions, that inconsistency must be resolved, either by correction of the executive director's letter or inclusion of an explanation as to why this isn't, in fact, an inconsistency. The not-for-profit organization's independent auditors should also read the entire annual report to identify any inconsistencies or discrepancies within the basic financial statements.

Interim Budgetary Reporting

The annual preparation and issuance of financial statement presented in accordance with GAAP would, by itself, generally not be considered sufficient for the day-to-day financial management of a midsize to large not-for-profit organization. First, financial statements presented in accordance with GAAP do not include a requirement to report any comparison of actual financial results with the organization's budget. Such a comparison provides an interesting insight as to how well management anticipates future financial activities through its budget and how well it executes its financial plan to "live" within the budget. Audit committee members should keep in mind that incentives to management to manipulate financial results take many forms. Although a not-for-profit organization does not report earnings per share as a financial performance indicator, certainly management is interested in knowing how the organization's actual results compare to its budget; accordingly, comparisons to budget may be an area that provides an incentive to management to manipulate financial results. For example, assume a large pledge for a contribution wasn't finalized until the week after the fiscal year-end, resulting in contribution revenues for the year being slightly overbudget instead of slightly underbudget. In this case, wouldn't there be an incentive for management to move that contribution back and report it in the earlier fiscal year? The point is not to suggest that most not-for-profit organization managers would do this, but to make you aware of these types of incentives and to stress the budget as an important performance indicator in the not-for-profit environment.

The second concept in this section deals with "interim" reporting in comparison with budgeted amounts. If an organization only compares budget to actual results after the end of the fiscal year, there is no time to make corrections to activities during the year to come closer to the budgeted amounts. These comparisons should be performed at least quarterly; but for midsize to larger not-for-profit organizations, monthly comparisons are probably more appropriate. These comparisons are important components of the internal control of the organization. The audit committee should be concerned with whether the organization's management regularly reports these amounts (along with explanations for variances and plans to remediate problems) to the governing board as a whole or to the budget or finance subcommittees of the governing board.

USERS OF NOT-FOR-PROFIT ORGANIZATION FINANCIAL STATEMENTS

An audit committee member might wonder why it is important to understand who are the primary readers and users of not-for-profit organization financial statements. Knowing the users of financial statements helps in making judgments about whether the financial statements are fairly stated in accordance with GAAP. Why is this the case? Basically, the preparation of financial statements involves many judgments, and many of these judgments concern the concept of what is "material" to the financial statements. Materiality is defined in another FASB Concepts Statement (No. 2, "Qualitative Characteristics of Accounting Information") as "the magnitude of an omission or misstatement of accounting information that, in light of the surrounding circumstances, makes it probable that the judgment of a reasonable person relying on the information would have been changed or influenced by the omission or misstatement." So materiality is based on the potential effect that the item being considered might have on a reader of the financial statements. Accordingly, it's a good idea for the committee members to have some perspective on the typical readers of not-for-profit organization financial statements.

In the environment of business organizations, specifically publicly traded companies, audit committee members can readily understand the primary users of financial statements. The audit committee members are elected to the governing board by shareholders, who have a keen interest in the financial reporting of the organization, since the financial performance reflected in the financial statements has an impact on the corporation's share price. Long-term debt holders and other creditors are also interested in whether the corporation has the ability to repay these debts in the future, and look to the financial statements as a primary means of making this assessment. In contrast, audit committee members of not-for-profit organizations have to ask themselves who are the primary users of the financial statements of not-for-profit organizations, because the answers are not quite as obvious as for public companies.

Looking again to the FASB's Concepts Statement No. 4, we find the following four groups that might be interested in the financial statements of not-for-profit organizations. These groups are not meant to be an all-inclusive listing of every type of individual who might read a not-for-profit organization's financial statements. Rather, it is meant to stimulate thought into what type of information may be important to various readers of a not-for-profit organization's financial statements, and to recognize that there are important differences between readers of not-for-profit financial statements and business organization financial statements.

Resource Providers

The most common resource providers to not-for-profit organizations are contributors. A contributor is, for example, very interested in knowing how much of the money received as contributions by not-for-profit organizations is used in its program activities, compared with how much is spent on general and administrative expenses, including fund-raising. A contributor making a long-term commitment for a capital program to a not-for-profit organization might also be interested in whether the organization is financially stable and whether it will still be in existence by the time that the capital program is completed. A contributor who imposes restrictions as to the purpose or timing of the use of a particular contribution may also be interested in seeing whether the organization has properly noted those restrictions in the financial statements.

A second type of resource provider includes those that are members of not-for-profit membership organizations. Examples include trade and professional associations, such as those for accountants, lawyers, physicians, engineers, and so on. Members are interested in knowing that their dues are being put to good programmatic use, to benefit them.

Several other types of resource providers that would be interested in a not-for-profit organization's financial statements include lenders, suppliers, and employees. Lenders and suppliers have an obvious interest in evaluating whether the not-for-profit organization will be able to repay any loans or credit extended as part of routine purchases of supplies. Employees are interested in knowing the financial soundness of the organization to determine such things as whether their payroll taxes, pension contributions, health insurance premiums, and so on are being paid timely. In addition, employees would be interested in knowing whether an organization has adequate resources to provide for salary increases in future years.

Constituents

Constituents are those who use and benefit from the services rendered by the not-for-profit organization. In the case of membership organizations, these may be the parties of the resource providers just described.

Governing and Oversight Bodies

These would include the not-for-profit organization's governing board, which may use the financial information provided in the financial statements to oversee and appraise the managers of the organization. Oversight bodies include national headquarters of organizations with local chapters, accrediting agencies, and agencies acting on behalf of contributors or constituents.

Managers

Managers of a not-for-profit organization are responsible for carrying out the policy mandates of governing bodies and managing the day-to-day operations of an organization. Managers include the managing executives appointed by the governing body, such as the executive director, and staff, such as fund-raising and program directors.

REGULATORY ENVIRONMENT OF NOT-FOR-PROFIT ORGANIZATIONS

One mistake that a not-for-profit organization audit committee member can easily make is to believe that not-for-profit organizations are relatively free of regulation. While it's true that these organizations are generally not publicly traded companies subject to the accounting and financial reporting requirements of the United States Securities and Exchange Commission, it would be incorrect to assume that there are no regulatory oversights. Audit committee members must not let themselves be blinded by the good works that a not-for-profit organization may be performing, if the same organization is running afoul of the regulations to which it is subject.

Let's look at two levels of regulation that would be common to most not-for-profit organizations: federal and state.

Federal Regulation

The first level of regulation to consider at the federal government level is that which is provided by the Internal Revenue Service (IRS). The IRS is the organization that grants a not-for-profit organization its exemption from federal income taxes. Does this mean that once an organization is granted such exemption it is free and clear of any IRS rules and regulations? Far from it. Let's consider a few areas by way of example:

- *Annual information return.* Not-for-profit organizations (except the very small ones) must file annual "information returns" with the IRS. This return is commonly referred to as Form 990, although there are some variations of it for small organizations and private foundations.

- *Unrelated business income tax.* To the extent that the organization earns income in ways not related to its exempt purpose, these earnings are subject to an unrelated business income tax, which must be paid to the IRS, fairly similar to a regular corporate income tax.

- *Payroll taxes.* While some not-for-profit organizations may be exempt from federal unemployment tax, generally this tax will apply, as well as all of the other payroll taxes, such as Social Security and Medicare taxes.

- *Prohibited or limited activities rules.* Depending on the Internal Revenue Section code under which a not-for-profit organization obtains its tax exemption, there are rules as to the types of activities an organization may engage in, particularly in the area of political activities and lobbying. In addition, the organization cannot be operated in such a manner that it privately benefits members of management or the governing board beyond normal amounts for compensation for services. Failure to follow these rules could result in monetary sanctions against the not-for-profit organization or, far worse, loss of its tax-exempt status.

The second level of federal regulation involves not-for-profit organizations that are recipients of federal awards, such as federal grants, loans, cooperative agreements, or contracts. These requirements apply whether the not-for-profit organization receives the federal award directly from a federal agency or indirectly, such as those passed through a state or local governmental entity or another not-for-profit organization. The requirements involve how the federal awards programs are managed, the various compliance requirements that must be adhered to in spending money under the various programs, and the annual audit and requirement requirements, which are commonly referred to as a *Single Audit.*

Keep in mind that not-for-profit organizations are, of course, subject to many other federal requirements, as are business enterprises, such as equal opportunity in employment and family leave requirements.

State Regulation

Not-for-profit organizations are also subject to regulation by states. These regulations will vary by state, but the following examples illustrate the complexity of some of these requirements:

- *Annual registration and reporting requirements.* Not-for-profit organizations are incorporated under the laws of a particular state. States generally have annual registration requirements using a form designed and issued by each particular state. Often, these registration forms must be accompanied by the financial statements of the not-for-profit organization. Based on the size of the organization, the financial statements may be required to be reviewed or audited by an independent auditor.

- *Raising funds in other states.* States generally have requirements that not-for-profit organizations incorporated in other states must register in order to solicit contributions within that state. Accordingly, not-for-profit organizations that raise funds in a number of states will need to comply with the various requirements of these states.

- *Oversight by state attorneys general or charities bureaus.* Again, depending on the structure of each individual statement, there will generally be a branch of the state government that has responsibility for monitoring the activities of the not-for-profit organizations incorporated or soliciting funds within that state.

- *Sales taxes.* A not-for-profit organization's tax-exempt status is unrelated to its responsibilities to collect and remit to state or local governments any sales taxes due on items or services that are sold by the not-for-profit organization.

The preceding points are certainly not meant to describe all of the regulations with which a not-for-profit organization must comply. Rather, they are meant to provide examples to not-for-profit audit committee members of the types of regulations to which these organizations are subject.

SUMMARY

This chapter provides a broad overview of not-for-profit organizations in general, and some of the financial reporting considerations of these organizations in particular. Understanding the context of the environment in which not-for-profit organizations operate is an important best practice for audit committee members of these organizations.

Chapter 2

Establishing an Audit Committee and Determining Its Charter

A not-for-profit organization that establishes an audit committee is already on the road to achieving best practices in accounting and financial reporting oversight. It's not enough to simply establish an audit committee, however; the key is to establish an *effective* audit committee. Leaving the determination of the functions of the audit committee to the committee's chair is not a useful way to establish an effective audit committee. Rather, the audit committee should adopt a written charter, which describes in considerable detail the responsibilities that the committee assumes and how it will operate.

There are several ways in which these charter activities can be documented. The governing board might create an audit committee and approve a charter that creates the committee and broadly defines its authority and responsibilities. The audit committee itself might then adopt its own bylaws that describe in more detail how the committee will operate in order to fulfill the responsibilities delegated to it by the governing board. Alternatively, the governing board may simply adopt a resolution creating the audit committee and instructing it to create its own bylaws. As a third alternative, the governing board may adopt a charter that includes all of these requirements for the audit committee, essentially serving as both a charter and bylaws.

More often, the best practice is for the governing board to adopt a broad charter creating the audit committee and broadly defining its roles and responsibilities. The audit committee itself would then adopt more detailed bylaws defining how it will carry out its responsibilities. This allows the governing board to define the areas that it believes are important (such as that the members of the audit committee be board members who are independent) while giving the audit committee flexibility in its operations (such as determining the minimum number of times that the audit committee will meet during the year.)

The format chosen, however, isn't nearly as important as coming to the best conclusion on all of the areas discussed in this chapter and ensuring that these conclusions are documented in an appropriately approved document.

Exhibit 2.1 provides an example of an audit committee charter. This example must be tailored to meet the individual needs of each particular not-for-profit organization that is drafting a charter. It would not be a best practice to adopt this example as a "boilerplate" charter without such tailoring.

Exhibit 2.1   Sample Audit Committee Charter

I. Legal Authority for the Audit Committee

The Board of Directors of the XYZ Not-for-Profit Organization, Inc. (hereafter, the "organization") by majority vote of the entire Board has established a standing Audit Committee that will be comprised of three members of the Board of Directors.

II. The primary duties of the Audit Committee include, but are not limited to, the following:

- Managing the selection, compensation, and terms of engagement of the organization's independent auditor.
- Assessing the independence of the organization's independent auditor.
- Reviewing the scope of the audit to be performed by the independent auditor.
- Overseeing management's review of the internal controls of the organization, including:
  - Internal controls over financial reporting
  - Internal audit activities
  - Fraud prevention and detection activities
- Reviewing the annual financial statements.
- Discussing the results of the audit with the independent auditor, including review of the plan of implementation for any recommendations provided by the independent auditor in a management letter.
- Monitoring management's processes for ensuring the organization's compliance with various laws, regulations, contracts, and grants.
- Providing an avenue for the receipt of anonymous and other complaints from employees and others regarding accounting, auditing internal control, or financial reporting matters.
- Providing a mechanism for open communications among management, the independent auditor, and the audit committee.
- Undertaking additional tasks requested by the Board of Directors.

III. Membership

The Chair of the Board of Directors shall propose to the entire Board of Directors for approval or rejection the names of three Directors for membership on the Audit Committee and shall also recommend one of them to be the chair of the Audit Committee. At least one, but to the extent possible, all members of the Audit Committee shall possess substantial financial or accounting experience and expertise. Audit Committee members must maintain their independence from the organization and must annually prepare and submit a conflicts-of-interest statement in accordance with the organization's requirements.

IV. Terms of Membership

Audit Committee members shall serve for a term of three years, with terms expiring on June 30, 20X1, 20X2, and 20X3. Audit Committee members may be reappointed to a maximum of one additional term. The Chair of the Audit Committee shall serve in that capacity until such time as his or her term expires or is replaced by the Board of Directors.

Exhibit 2.1   Sample Audit Committee Charter (continued)

V. Meetings

The Audit Committee shall meet four times each year or more frequently as circumstances dictate. The Chair of the Audit Committee shall prepare a written agenda in advance of each meeting. The Audit Committee shall submit on a timely basis minutes of each of its meetings to the Board of Directors for its review. Members shall attend meetings in person and may not designate an individual to represent them in any voting capacity at any meeting for which they cannot attend.

VI. Outside Counsel and Advisors

The Audit Committee shall have the right to engage outside counsel and other advisors to assist in the performance of its duties if it deems necessary.

VII. Annual Report

The Audit Committee shall prepare a report delineating its activities for the annual period ending each June 30. This report shall be sent within 90 to the Board of Directors

---

Why are written charters (or bylaws) necessary to guide an audit committee? There are several reasons:

- Audit committee members will have a clear understanding of their responsibilities and the expectations that are placed on them.
- The full governing board will know what the functions that the audit committee is assuming. This will prevent any misunderstanding as the audit committee's role.
- The functions of the audit committee have a better chance to remain consistent in future years as individual members rotate on and off of the audit committee.
- In the not-for-profit organization environment, there is currently no set of requirements defined for audit committee, such as those required by the Sarbanes-Oxley Act for public companies. Because the roles and activities of the audit committee can be customized for each organization, a clear statement of these roles and activities is necessary in order to define them.
- Drafting the charter and bylaws will force the audit committee and the governing board to deal with specific issues as to the functions and composition of the committee.

This final point can't be overemphasized. The chapter is laid out in such a way to facilitate this decision-making process. The remainder of this chapter suggests several areas that are recommended to be covered as part of the audit committee's charter. As each area is addressed, the pros and cons of various options for how the committee's roles and activities are defined by the charter are discussed. This chapter also discusses several of the more narrowly focused areas that should be covered in the audit committee charter or bylaws, specifically:

- Charter and bylaws review
- Audit committee members
- Number of audit committee meetings
- Meeting attendance
- Minutes of meetings
- Designation of an audit committee chair
- Designation of an audit committee secretary
- Terms of audit committee appointments
- Staggering audit committee terms
- Annual review and reporting of audit committee activities
- Ability to hire outside counsel and other advisors
- Conflicts-of-interest statements

Several of the functions and activities of the audit committee that should be mentioned in the committee's charters or bylaws require more detailed analysis; accordingly, these topics are covered in subsequent chapters of this book. These functions and activities include:

- Assigning responsibilities as to the not-for-profit organization's internal control over financial reporting.
- Understanding the risks of fraud, and management's plans to address those risks.
- Establishing communications with "whistleblowers."
- Communicating with management regarding accounting, financial reporting, and internal control issues.
- Understanding the internal audit function
- Acquiring audit services from an independent auditor.
- Reviewing the independent auditor's audit plan and approach.
- Reviewing audit results, draft financial statements, and management letter.

After addressing each of these areas, the body of the audit committee charter and/or bylaws will essentially be drafted. All that will remain for the audit committee to do is commit its decisions on these areas to writing; a draft charter and/or bylaws will result.

CHARTER AND BYLAWS REVIEW

The audit committee charter and/or bylaws should ideally state that on some periodic basis the governing board or audit committee should review the audit committee charter (governing board) or bylaws (audit committee, with governing board approval) to see if there are any areas that need to be revised. This review is best done annually, but a longer time frame might be appropriate, such as every two years or, stretching it a bit, every five years. Obviously, some change in circumstances (such as a new state law that establishes audit committee requirements for not-for-profit organizations incorporated within that state) may necessitate the charter or bylaws of an audit committee to be changed more quickly.

As part of this review, the audit committee should consider how it would actually become aware of new requirements relating to its functions, and establish a requirement for management to advise the audit committee of changes in the regulator environment that might have an impact on the committee's responsibilities. There are other parties that might impose such requirements. For example, audits of organizations that are recipients of federal awards programs and that are subject to the federal Single Audits Amendments Act are required to be performed in accordance with *Government Auditing Standards,* which are established by the federal Government Accountability Office (GAO). It's conceivable that at some future date some of the requirements of the Sarbanes-Oxley Act may be imposed on these federal awards recipients and their independent auditors. An audit committee inquiry into the not-for-profit organization's independent auditor as to changes in the regulatory environment might also be useful, not only in bringing these types of matters to light, but in bringing them to light in a timely manner so that their implementation can be accomplished in a methodical, professional manner.

In other words, the best practice to keep an audit committee's charter and bylaws up to date really has two components: providing that the documents be periodically reviewed and updated, and setting up a mechanism through which the audit committee members will know when a change to their charter or bylaws is necessary or desirable.

AUDIT COMMITTEE MEMBERS

The following considerations should be made in determining the composition of the members of the audit committee.

Number of Members

The first matter to decide is how many audit committee members there should be. Ideally, this number will be an odd one, so that in the event of any contentious votes, the committee wouldn't be stymied by a tie. For most small to midsized not-for-profit organizations, three audit committee members would generally be sufficient. For very large not-for-profit organizations or not-for-profit organizations with very large governing boards, or if it is anticipated that not all committee members will make all meetings, it may make sense to increase this number to five. Any more than five would probably result in a less effective committee because each individual member's influence on the committee would become too diluted. Fewer than three committee members is not practical, since having two members may result in the voting issues previously described; and one member wouldn't exactly meet the definition of a "committee," and would, in any case, be too onerous for one individual to handle.

BEST PRACTICE

Three to five audit committee members is usually the optimal number for best results.

Audit Committee Members Who Are Also Governing Board Members

The Sarbanes-Oxley Act for public companies specifies that audit committee members should be directors, so they do not have much flexibility. In contrast, not-for-profit organizations have the option of choosing whether they want the audit committee members to all be governing board members, as well. Certainly, having all members of the audit committee also members of the governing board is the more classical approach to audit committee membership, in that the audit committee is then truly a subcommittee of the governing board. In the most common situations found in not-for-profit organizations, this would likely be considered the best practice to adopt. That said, this classical approach may not always work with some not-for-profit organizations, in which case the following two alternatives may also be considered in order to ensure the best and most productive membership on the audit committee.

Some not-for-profit organizations view the governing board as part of the managers of the organization, in that they can be the ultimate decision makers on matters affecting the organization. Therefore, to achieve a level of greater "independence" (described in the next section), some not-for-profit organizations recruit audit committee members who are not members of the governing board. These audit committee members operate completely independently of any other management decision-making process in the organization. If the governing board of a particular not-for-profit is heavily involved in managing the day-to-day affairs of the organization, this approach may make sense. In these cases, it may be difficult to separate management from the governing board; and having outside, nongoverning board members on the audit committee may further remove the audit committee from management, which might be helpful. Otherwise, this may be a little extreme in carrying out the notion of independence. One downside to this approach is that the audit committee members have no official "standing" (read: "power") within the not-for-profit organization. Audit committee members who are also members of the governing board have an official role related to the organization, which is their ability to vote on issues as full governing board members. Such standing does not exist for the audit committee composed of nongoverning board members, who then must rely on the governing board entirely to act, where necessary, on its recommendations. Whereas an audit committee is always dependent on whether the full governing board will accept its recommendations, having no governing board members on the audit committee exacerbates this situation.

A third alternative is to have the audit committee composed of both governing board members and nongoverning board members. This alternative may be useful when none (or not enough of) the governing board members have the necessary accounting and financial expertise to properly fulfill their responsibilities as audit committee members. This alternative is a useful technique to obtain that expertise, while still having governing board members with an active role on the audit committee. To the extent that there are some independence concerns with the governing board as a whole, this alternative also provides some measure of additional independence to the audit committee since not all of its members will be governing board members.

BEST PRACTICE

Audit committee members should be members of the not-for-profit organization's governing board.

Independence of Audit Committee Members

In terms of best practices, audit committee members virtually have to be independent in order for the audit committee to have credibility and function effectively. Sarbanes-Oxley has what, in my opinion, is as good a definition of independence for audit committee members as any, and the best approach would simply be to adopt its requirements. Sarbanes-Oxley defines independence as follows:

> In order to be considered independent . . . a member of an audit committee . . . may not, other than is his or her capacity as a member of the audit committee, the board of directors, or any other board committee—(i) accept any consulting, advisory, or other compensatory fee from the issuer, or (ii) be an affiliated person of the issuer or any subsidiary thereof.

For purposes of applying this definition, it is necessary to substitute "not-for-profit organization" for "issuer." Accordingly, audit committee members should not be members of management and should not, effectively, be working for the not-for-profit organization in some other capacity. In the rare case where not-for-profit organizations compensate their board members, such compensation would not impair an audit committee member's independence. Interestingly, audit committee members are not precluded from serving on other subcommittees of the governing board.

The definition also requires audit committee members to be independent of subsidiaries. Although not-for-profit organizations don't always call affiliated organizations "subsidiaries," it would seem prudent to require that audit committee members also be independent of affiliated organizations, as defined by generally accepted accounting principles (GAAP) for not-for-profit organizations. In some instances, because of overlapping boards or other factors, not-for-profit organizations can be so interrelated that it would be best to have audit committee members independent of all of these types of interrelated or affiliated organizations.

BEST PRACTICE

Audit committee members should be independent of the not-for-profit organization.

Audit Committee Member Skill Sets

Not-for-profit organizations should not assume that the best practice for skills required of the audit committee is that the members be composed entirely of experts in accounting, auditing, and financial reporting. First, this is probably not a practical recommendation since the audit committee members are likely to be a subset of the governing board (as just discussed), meaning that it would be unusual to have three or more governing board members with these skills who could be made part of the audit committee. In addition, other subcommittees of the governing board (such as the finance, budget, or investment committees) would also compete for these types of skills for their members. Conversely, it seems impractical and unwise to expect an audit committee to assume its significant responsibilities if none of its members has experience in accounting, auditing, or financial reporting. Between these two extremes is the best practice: having at least one member of the audit committee with experience in accounting, auditing, and financial reporting.

In addition to having these required skills represented by at least one audit committee member, there is a secondary benefit to not having all of the audit committee members with accounting and auditing backgrounds. Sometimes individuals from different professions and disciplines can bring a broader perspective to the audit committee tasks and responsibilities. Many of you can probably recall being in a meeting where a novice to the topic being discussed asks a question that would be too "obvious" for the experts to ask, and the question results in some important facts or disclosures coming to light, which never would have, had the novice question not been asked. Nonfinancial members of an audit committee can bring different perspectives and viewpoints to the committee, which can result in important contributions to the committee's work.

Let's assume that the best practice being adopted is to require at least one audit committee member to be a financial expert. (This practice would be consistent with that required for public companies by Sarbanes-Oxley.) What characteristics and experiences would make an individual a financial expert? A good way to start this investigation is to consider the rules adopted by the United States Securities and Exchange Commission (SEC) for defining financial experts as contemplated by Sarbanes-Oxley. Remember that there is no need for a not-for-profit organization to meet the requirements established by the SEC as to this definition of the financial expert. The attributes discussed here are those adopted by the SEC after public deliberations and commentary, and they are being listed as the best-case scenario in identifying a financial expert, rather than implying that a not-for-profit organization's audit committee financial expert must meet all of these criteria. In other words, read these attributes as a guide, rather than as an indelible checklist.

The SEC rules define an audit committee financial expert as a person who has the following attributes:

> An understanding of generally accepted accounting principles and financial statements.

This attribute is fairly straightforward, although the term "understanding" certainly can encompass a wide range of skills.

> The ability to assess the general application of such principles in connection with the accounting for estimates, accruals, and reserves.

Since the application of estimates, accruals, and reserves is needed in almost all cases to prepare financial statements in accordance with GAAP, this requirement is practically a subset of the first item. Examples of these types of items at a not-for-profit organization might involve estimates for the amount of donor pledges that will be uncollectible, estimates as to liability for the unfavorable outcome of litigation against the not-for-profit organization, and the write-off of some portion of a capital asset because the asset has lost its usefulness or value to the not-for-profit organization (the asset has become "impaired," in the correct accounting jargon). The estimate of the liability for medical malpractice for a not-for-profit health care organization is also a good example of a significant estimate that could have a significant impact on the amounts reported within a set of financial statements.

This requirement doesn't mean that the audit committee financial expert must have an in-depth knowledge of how these amounts are calculated. Rather, the requirement means that the audit committee financial expert should be aware that the calculation of estimates, accruals, and reserves plays an important part in preparing financial statements in accordance with GAAP, hence should have a sufficient knowledge to understand these calculations as they apply to the particular not-for-profit organization.

> Experience in preparing, auditing, analyzing, or evaluating financial statements that present a breadth and level of complexity of accounting issues that are generally comparable to the breadth and complexity of issues that can reasonably be expected to be raised by the . . . financial statements, or experience actively supervising one or more persons engaged in such activities.

Several components of this attribute need to be looked at separately. First, the audit committee financial expert does not necessarily need to have experience in preparing or auditing financial statements. An individual who has experience in analyzing financial statements may also have the necessary skills to be the audit committee financial expert. Second, regardless of how the skills are gained, they should be comparable to activities in the not-for-profit organization. For example, experience as the treasurer of a local student soccer association might not adequately prepare an individual to be the audit committee financial expert of a major college or university. Finally, the SEC acknowledged that these skills may also be obtained by actively supervising individuals who had more direct experience in this area. Not-for-profit organizations seeking to generally comply with these requirements should also give credit for such supervisory experience. A word of caution, however: Determine whether the supervision was hands-on or remote, to identify how much the individual really understood about the processes they were supervising.

An understanding of internal controls and procedures for financial reporting.

An entire chapter of this book is devoted to helping audit committee members understand internal control and its role in financial reporting. This SEC requirement affirms the importance of the audit committee's understanding of this area. It's interesting to note that the SEC's original requirement was for "experience" in internal control, rather than just an "understanding," as reflected in the final requirements. Obviously, it would be harder to find individuals with such experience, rather than understanding. The SEC concluded in the end that understanding was more important than experience in this area.

An understanding of audit committee functions.

This requirement might be even more important in the world of not-for-profit audit committees because, as was stated previously, there is no concrete set of rules for not-for-profit organization audit committees to follow. Rather, these audit committees and their governing boards establish the functions that will be performed for their respective organizations. The audit committee financial expert should understand these functions, as should all audit committee members.

In addition to defining the preceding attributes for an audit committee's financial expert, the SEC also specified how such attributes could be acquired. For the purpose of applying these requirements, an individual must have acquired these attributes through any one or more of the following:

- Education and experience as a principal financial officer, principal accounting officer, controller, public accountant, or auditor, or experience in one or more positions that involve the performance of similar functions;
- Experience actively supervising a principal financial officer, principal accounting officer, controller, public accountant, auditor, or person performing such functions;
- Experience overseeing or assessing the performance of companies or public accountants with respect to the preparation, auditing or evaluation of financial statements; or
- Other relevant experience.

In reading down this list, it may have seemed that it would be very difficult to meet these requirements—until reaching the fourth bullet, which makes it sound as if almost any other type of experience would qualify. For public companies, there are several limitations on the "other relevant experience" requirement that are beyond the scope of this book.

For not-for-profit organizations desiring to include an audit committee financial expert as a member of their audit committee, the fortunate part of this analysis is that these requirements are discussed only to assist in providing a perspective and basis for identifying an audit committee's financial expert. It becomes more important to consider the substance of these requirements, to determine which ones are relevant or important to the particular not-for-profit organization, and to base a search for such a committee member on the results of these considerations. Once an individual is found who is a good fit for a particular organization, the governing board and its audit committee do not need to agonize over whether the person meets all of the SEC's requirements, since they are not required to do so. This flexibility means the committee does not have to exclude individuals who might possess great financial experience and who would be a real asset to the audit committee, even though this might mean that not every "t" was crossed or "i" dotted in complying with the aforementioned requirements.

BEST PRACTICE

At least one audit committee member should be an audit committee financial expert. Individuals with nonfinancial skill sets can be good audit committee members.

NUMBER OF AUDIT COMMITTEE MEETINGS

The audit committee's charter or bylaws should make mention of the number of meetings that the committee anticipates it will have during the year. Ideally, the dates for these meeting can be established at the beginning of each year to avoid as many scheduling conflicts as possible. As a frame of reference, a public company might have four audit committee meeting during the year, timed to coincide with the company's announcement of its quarterly earnings. In the not-for-profit environment, there is no such concrete driver as to the frequency of meetings, so some careful consideration is warranted.

The first consideration is the schedule of the governing board meetings. If the not-for-profit organization has opted to have the audit committee members be members of the governing board, which is the recommended approach, then it certainly makes sense to have the audit committee meetings on the same days as the governing board meetings. If this can be accomplished, it would also be beneficial to have the audit committee meetings prior to the full governing board meeting, particularly when the audit committee will be reporting on its activities to the governing board. (For larger organizations with more formal board and committee meeting settings, this may prove to be a little aggressive, particularly if the report of the audit committee to the governing board is written or done by a slide show.)

The second consideration is the timing of the financial reporting and audit activities that the not-for-profit organization's audit committee will be discussing and addressing. We'll be addressing these topics in much greater depth later in this book, but for now it's sufficient to understand that meetings should be held to discuss the audit plan with the independent auditor, to review the draft financial statements prior to issuance, and, finally, to meet to discuss the auditor's management comment letter, which contains the auditor's suggestions for improvements to the organization's financial operations. The smaller the organization, the shorter the time span over which these three meetings will occur; the larger the organization, the longer the time span over which these three meeting will occur. In smaller organizations, the audit of financial statements by an independent auditor might be completed in a couple of weeks. For larger organizations, the audit of financial statements may occur over a period of several months. Assuming that the discussion of the audit plan will occur before the audit is performed (an easy best practice to identify!) the time between meetings will clearly be impacted by the time that it takes the independent auditor to perform the audit.

The preceding paragraphs point to at least three audit committee meetings anticipated for most not-for-profit organization audit committees. However, there are numerous other tasks and responsibilities that the audit committee may find itself undertaking, and it is very likely that at least one additional meeting will need to be held. It would make the most sense to schedule this additional meeting as evenly spaced as possible between the audit conclusion meeting held to discuss the management commentary letter and the audit planning meeting for the next year's audit. Usually, this is the longest period of time when there would otherwise be no meetings. Audit committees may find it very helpful to "check in" with the organization as to accounting and financial reporting issues during this "off-season" in the financial reporting process. (Later in this book we'll also discuss the audit committee's role in internal control.) This off-season meeting might also be an appropriate time to have the audit committee review an update on the status of any internal control improvements that were intended to be implemented during the year.

The guidelines just given attempt only to address the most common situations likely to be encountered; there is no hard-and-fast rule as to the right number of meetings that a particular not-for-profit audit committee should plan on holding. For example, if the governing board of the not-for-profit organization meets six times a year, there is certainly nothing wrong with the audit committee meeting each time that there is a governing board meeting. If the governing board meets monthly, perhaps the audit committee could convene its meetings to coincide with every other governing board meeting.

Planning meetings in advance is certainly the most logical way for an audit committee to function, but there provision also needs to be made for the committee to meet on an ad hoc basis, if necessary, because of specific events or needs that arise.

BEST PRACTICE

Four audit committee meetings per year, with additional meetings for unforeseen circumstances as needed.

MEETING ATTENDANCE

Two questions should be considered with regard to audit committee member attendance at meetings. First, should committee members be permitted to attend meetings by telephone? Second, should audit committee members be permitted to send a designee to represent them at a committee meeting?

Generally, the audit committee should permit members to "attend" meetings via telephone. However, attendance in this manner should be the exception to standard operating practices and therefore limited. Certainly if an audit committee is meeting and one member can't attend in person because of a conflict in schedule or travel, attendance by telephone is certainly preferable to not attending at all. This is particularly true when an audit committee consists of only three members. On the other hand, a member who consistently doesn't attend meetings in person because it is simply easier to phone in is probably not serving the committee in the best capacity possible. Making it clear to audit committee members prior to their appointment that they are expected to attend all meetings in person can avoid the embarrassing situation of having to discuss poor meeting attendance with a particular audit committee member.

One very effective way of handling ad hoc meetings that need to quickly address a specific issue is to hold the committee meeting via a teleconference call. The operating practices of a not-for-profit organization's audit committee should permit this type of meeting to occur. However, it is not recommended that this format be used for the audit committee's regularly scheduled meetings. There is too much value in face-to-face discussions and conversations to hold regular meeting via teleconference.

The second meeting attendance issue has to do with whether an audit committee member should be permitted to designate another individual to attend meetings on his or her behalf. Best practices would not permit such representation by a designee. Audit committee members are made members of this committee because of the various types of expertise that they can bring to the audit committee's operations. This experience cannot be obtained from a member's representative. True, such a representative may have more knowledge than the committee member him- or herself, but this will not be the usual case. In addition, audit committee members take on various responsibilities when they become audit committee members, and those responsibilities should remain with them. Furthermore, audit committee members—assuming they are also members of the governing board—are generally covered by a not-for-profit organization's director's and officer's insurance policy. (Audit committee members should confirm this fact, as well as that such insurance is carried; they should not take this for granted.) The legal implications of using a member's designated representative are beyond the scope of this book, but suffice to say it would definitely cloud these legal liability issues.

One exception to this practice to consider, however, is to allow an audit committee member who is unable to attend a meeting to send a representative to the meeting solely in the capacity as a meeting observer. This individual could then later brief the audit committee member on the substance of the meeting; but the "stand-in" would have no authority to vote on issues or to participate in discussions. Frankly, this approach is not the best, since the absent committee member's input to the meeting will be missed. Still, there may be a unique circumstance beyond a committee member's control that might make this an acceptable practice.

BEST PRACTICE

In-person attendance by all audit committee members, with infrequent exceptions made for call-in attendance.

MINUTES OF MEETINGS

It's important for the audit committee to maintain a record of its activities conducted at its meetings, and the traditional manner to accomplish this is through the keeping of minutes of meetings. These minutes serve as a formal record of the activities of the audit committee and are important in that they document how the audit committee is (presumably) fulfilling its responsibilities. The secretary of the audit committee (discussed shortly) or other appropriate individual should be responsible for preparing a draft of the audit committee meeting minutes. The draft minutes should then be reviewed and approved by the committee members. Usually, the audit committee members will approve (or suggest changes) to the minutes at the subsequent committee meeting.

The style of the audit committee's minutes is something that the secretary or minute-taker and the committee members will need to agree on based on the needs of the particular not-for-profit organization. What is meant by "style"? It's really the extent of the details to include in the minutes. For example, some committees and organizations prefer minutes that summarize their activities at a very high level and may focus on formal resolutions or actions taken by the committee, rather than the discussions that preceded those actions or resolutions. At the other extreme, some audit committees' minutes provide an almost verbatim transcript of the discussions of the committee members, along with the committee's actions and resolutions. Proponents of the first approach would argue that too much detail in the minutes stifles discussion among the committee members. Proponents of the latter would argue that it is important to document the individual discussions and points of views of the committee members, in order to clearly document that the committee was diligent in fulfilling its responsibilities. The most common approach (again, there is no general right or wrong approach) would be for the minutes to state the actions or resolutions of the committee, along with a summary of the discussions that surrounded those actions and resolutions—a kind of hybrid approach.

BEST PRACTICE

Minutes should be taken for each audit committee meeting, and those minutes should be reviewed and approved by the audit committee members.

DESIGNATION OF COMMITTEE CHAIR

One of the audit committee members should be designated as the chair of the committee. A chair is needed to serve as the focal point, to ensure that the committee runs properly, including initiating meetings and presiding over those meetings. The chair holds power in directing the operations of the committee, but in terms of voting, he or she has the same voting authority as all of the other committee members. Whereas a charter and bylaws attempt to standardize an audit committee's operations, the style of the chair will likely have an impact on how the committee functions. An aggressive or assertive chair is likely to steer the audit committee to a more active role in the accounting and financial reporting of the not-for-profit organization. A more passive chair is likely to ensure that the audit committee meets its responsibilities, but does not become active in areas not specified in its charter or by-laws.

Other than recognizing that an overly aggressive or overly passive individual may not be the best fit for the chair of an audit committee, there is really no best practice as to chair style, although the more aggressive approach is likely to have a greater impact on the not-for-profit organization's accounting and financial reporting than the passive. The best practice for selection of the audit committee chair involves who will decide who the committee chair will be. There are two basic approaches:

- When the governing board appoints members to the audit committee, it can designate the individual who will serve as chair of the committee.
- The audit committee members can elect the chair of the committee.

As usual, there are pros and cons to each approach; that said, having the governing board designate the chair of the audit committee would have to get the nod as the best practice. Particularly if an audit committee is composed of three members, an election by the audit committee members is awkward, especially if more than one individual is interested in being the chair. While a committee might be more motivated to support and work with a chair that it has elected, given the small number of audit committee members typically found on audit committees, there are just not enough voters to make this a meaningful process. Designation of the chair by the governing board eliminates these election difficulties. In addition, given that the audit committee is being given specific tasks and responsibilities by the governing board, and that the chair will have an integral role in executing these tasks and undertaking these responsibilities, it is best left to the governing board to make the appointment of the chair of the committee.

BEST PRACTICE

The governing board should designate an audit committee member to serve as chair of the audit committee.

DESIGNATION OF A COMMITTEE SECRETARY

In the most typical situations, not-for-profit organization audit committees do not have separate staff individuals to attend to their administrative needs. These administrative tasks often fall to the staff of the not-for-profit organization. In most cases, the administrative needs of the governing board are met in the same way. Therefore, it can be very helpful to designate an individual to serve as the secretary of the audit committee. The role of the secretary should not be viewed solely in as an administrative or traditional type of function. It certainly includes these aspects, but the secretary should also be viewed as the official record keeper of the committee. It's clear from the numerous topics covered in this book that audit committee members take on a wide range of responsibilities related to their role as audit committee members. Making sure that their activities are planned, scheduled, and documented in a professional, methodical manner will serve as an important confirmation that their activities were conducted in the appropriate manner.

Typical tasks that will need to be performed by an audit committee's secretary include:

- Planning and scheduling audit committee meetings.
- Distributing agendas and advance reading materials to committee members prior to meetings.
- Preparing minutes of the audit committee meetings.
- Drafting the annual report (discussed later) on audit committee activities.
- Maintaining records of committee members' conflicts-of-interest statements (also discussed later).
- Following up on matters discussed at committee meetings that require additional information to be provided to the committee by others, such as management or the independent auditors.

Unless these functions are assigned to a particular individual, it is all too likely that administrative foul-ups will occur, hindering the audit committee's ability to perform its functions.

Some of the functions of the committee secretary will require a fairly good understanding of the topics that the committee is reviewing and discussing, the secretary should have a high level of accounting and financial knowledge. For example, drafting minutes often will require the secretary to have a basic understanding of the accounting topics being discussed, or the minutes will reflect merely verbatim statements rather than a coherent summarization of the discussions that occurred at the meetings.

BEST PRACTICE

A secretary possessing sufficient knowledge should be assigned to the audit committee to facilitate and document its meetings and other activities.

TERMS OF AUDIT COMMITTEE APPOINTMENTS

The audit committee's charter or bylaws should specify the length of member appointments. Having a fixed-term appointment is recommended, as it provides a built-in mechanism for rotation of audit committee members. Rotation ensures that current members won't get "stale" and start performing their roles in an automatic manner. It also provides the opportunity for new members to join the audit committee, bringing fresh ideas that the committee as a whole may find very beneficial.

In a practical sense, a fixed-term appointment can make it much easier for an audit committee member who wishes to step down from the audit committee; it also makes it easier for a governing board that makes appointments to the audit committee and desires to remove an existing member. It is much smoother and less uncomfortable for all parties involved if these changes can be made at the expiration of a defined term. New committee members will also have an idea about the length of the commitment they are making to the audit committee.

That being said, two questions need to be addressed. First, how long should the standard term be for members appointed to the audit committee? Second, can audit committee members serve more than one term, and can multiple terms be served consecutively?

The length of appointment to the audit committee is a tough question to answer in general for not-for-profit organizations. A good case could be made to have the term be for as little as one year. Or a term as long as four years might also seem reasonable. Less than one year would be ridiculous, and more than four years is probably far too long a commitment for a voluntary committee member to make to the not-for-profit organization. In addition, the benefits of defined terms diminish if the terms last more than four years. The size of the audit committee should also be factored into term length. If there are three committee members, the term should be at least three years so that (assuming a staggering of terms as described shortly) not more than one member changes every year. For larger committees, shorter terms would not have as significant an impact on the member rotations on and off of the committee.

The question of whether an audit committee member should be permitted to serve more than one term is another that should be addressed by the charter or by-laws of the audit committee. The more common question is whether an audit committee member can be reappointed for an additional term or terms without a break in their service to the committee. Generally, there is nothing wrong with enabling consecutive reappointments to the audit committee. If a member is serving the committee well, and the governing board is satisfied with his or her service, it would do more harm than good to force this individual to relinquish his or her audit committee membership. Enabling reappointment does, however, diminish some of the benefits of the defined terms; at the same time, it does enable the not-for-profit organization to have the best of both worlds in many respects—that is, an opportunity to change committee members at a fixed point in time, while at the same time enabling good committee members to continue to serve.

Whether reappointment to more than one term is permitted is an additional question to address. The answer to this is somewhat dependent on the length of the terms that are chosen. For example, if a four-year term is chosen, reappointment to only one additional term would make sense since eight total years is a long time to serve on the audit committee, and the not-for-profit organization and governing board would probably be well served by limiting the reappointment to one term. On the other hand, if the audit committee member term is set at two years, reappointment to more than one additional term would be an acceptable practice in most circumstances. Four years is not so long that a person will become too "stale" to be effective, and an additional two-year term might be desirable in most circumstances.

Finally, there is the question of whether audit committee members who come off the audit committee yet remain on the governing board can be reappointed to the audit committee after a break from their audit committee membership. If an individual is willing to serve again, and the governing board was so pleased with their first term of service that they are willing to reappoint that individual to a second period of service, there doesn't seem to be much of a downside for doing so, either for the committee member, the governing board, or the not-for-profit organization.

BEST PRACTICE

Audit committee members should be appointed for fixed terms, generally from two to four years, with opportunity for reappointment.

STAGGERING AUDIT COMMITTEE MEMBER TERMS

The audit committee of a not-for-profit organization handles a number of complex issues and has a great deal of responsibility to the governing board in meeting its mission. In addition, many of the issues that the audit committee addresses recur from year to year. For these and a number of other reasons, there is a benefit to having membership continuity on the audit committee. What this means is that audit committees that have established finite terms of appointment, as discussed in the previous section, should avoid all of the terms expiring at the same time. Instead, the terms should expire on a staggered basis, in a manner to achieve the greatest level of continuity possible. For example, an audit committee that has a member term of three years and three members on the committee should arrange to have one term expire each year. In this way, at least two committee members will have been members in the prior year. This would seem to be the minimum level of continuity to be achieved. Not-for-profit organizations and their governing boards should balance the size of the audit committee, length of terms, and the term-staggering strategy to maximize continuity of members to the greatest extent possible, while still maintaining a healthy rotation of members.

BEST PRACTICE

Stagger the expiring terms of audit committee members to achieve continuity among committee members.

ANNUAL REVIEW AND REPORTING OF AUDIT COMMITTEE ACTIVITIES

An audit committee can easily fall into a routine (some might call it a rut), and repetitively perform its duties year after year giving little thought to what changes should be made to its functions or operations to make them more effective. Granted, the changes being forced on public company audit committees by the Sarbanes-Oxley Act, as well as the many accounting and financial reporting problems that continue to come to light, have caused many, if not all, governing boards and audit committees at all types of organizations (other than public companies) to examine their procedures and responsibilities to make sure that they are effective. These factors are likely to be some of the reasons that you are reading this book. These changes are real and, in the long run, should prove helpful to the integrity of the financial reporting process.

However, following the adoption of a new charter or bylaws, and taking the consensus view of the best practices for a particular not-for-profit organization's audit committee, it is not enough to say, "Well, we're glad that's behind us," believing that the audit committee's future functions and activities are now set in stone. Best practices are not static. Rather, they are the practices that, based upon knowledge of the facts and circumstances that exist at a particular point in time, are considered the best to implement. Effective implementation of best practices involves a periodic review of how the current practices and activities are working—that is, asking, are they meeting the objectives of the audit committee as defined by the governing board?

In order to facilitate the periodic review of the audit committee's activities, it's first necessary to establish the time period for which the review will be performed. It's pretty clear that the period covered should be one year, but the real question is, should a calendar year be used, or should the not-for-profit organization's fiscal year be used, or should the annual review encompass some other annual period? First, there doesn't appear to be a compelling reason to select the calendar year period for this review. Second, the not-for-profit organization's fiscal year-end may be the worst choice for an annual review of an audit committee's activities, because the fiscal year-end is in the middle of the audit committee's natural cycle of activities. For example, the audit committee is probably reviewing the independent auditor's audit plan before the fiscal year-end, and the results of the audit after the year-end. Using the fiscal year-end in this example would not allow the audit committee to look at its performance relative to the financial reporting process as a whole.

The ideal period to select for the annual review is at the end of some period when all of the activities of the committee relating to a particular fiscal year of the not-for-profit organization have been completed. This may be several months after the organization's fiscal year-end. The important point is that the review should be performed soon enough after the fiscal year-end so that the previous year is still fresh in the audit committee members' minds, enabling them to conduct a meaningful review. At the same time, this leaves sufficient time before the subsequent year's activities begin, so that there will be enough time to implement any changes that the audit committee desires to make. For example, if the audit committee is asking the governing board to change the audit committee's charter, time will be needed to draft the changes, have them reviewed, and have them approved by the governing board. If the governing board doesn't meet very frequently, sufficient time must be allowed so that the changes make it on the governing board's meeting calendar. For calendar year-end not-for-profit organizations, the review period may be from July 1 to June 30. For not-for-profit organizations with fiscal year-ends of June 30, the calendar year may be the most appropriate time period for the audit committee's annual review.

This best practice really comprises two parts. First, a very effective way to begin the review of the committee's activities is with a written report that summarizes the audit committee's activities for the year being reviewed. Therefore, the first part of this best practice is to prepare an annual summary of audit committee activities. This report should be prepared not only for the audit committee's use, however; it is also an effective way to formally communicate the audit committee's activities to the governing board.

As noted previously, not-for-profit organization audit committees seldom have their own staffs, so the report draft is likely to be prepared by the audit committee secretary (or management or other staff member, if a secretary has not otherwise been designated) and approved by the audit committee. While it's true that the audit committee's activities should be documented in meeting minutes, the audit committee's annual report should summarize the committee's activities for the year in such a way that the reader does not have to sift through detailed minutes to understand the activities of the committee for the year.

As with taking meeting minutes, discussed previously, there can also be a wide range of detail included in the audit committee's annual report. Some reports may be very brief, others more detailed. The important characteristic is that the level of detail be sufficient to enable the reader to understand precisely the formal activities and conclusions reached by the audit committee and the time frames over which they occurred. For example, if the independent auditor discussed a particular risk of fraud with the audit committee, the fact that the discussion took place should be listed as an activity of the audit committee in its annual report.

Upon the approval of the draft audit committee annual report by the committee members, it should be sent to the governing board to serve as a formal notification of the activities of the audit committee for the year.

The second part of this best practice is to use the audit committee's annual report as a starting point for performing an annual self-examination of the audit committee's activities and the effectiveness of its manner of functioning. Some of the topic areas to consider for coverage include whether:

- The audit committee had a positive impact on the accounting and financial reporting practices of the not-for-profit organization.
- The relationship between the audit committee and independent auditor is a healthy one, which encourages the free flow of information and ideas between the two.
- The level of involvement of the audit committee with the accounting and financial reporting operations of the not-for-profit organization was appropriate.
- The chair of the committee functioned effectively and led the committee while utilizing the experience and input of each of the other audit committee members to the fullest extent possible.
- Any charter or bylaws requirements or limitations had a negative effect on the audit committee's operations and whether the charter or bylaws were in need of amendment.
- The relationship of the audit committee and the governing board is appropriate, with good communications between the two, including a clear definition of the responsibilities given to the audit committee by the governing board.
- The relationship of the audit committee and management is good—again, with good communications between the two.
- Any administrative improvements can be made, such as the timeliness of receiving meeting materials in advance and whether audit committee minutes are being prepared to the committee's satisfaction.
- The action items that resulted from the prior year's assessment of the audit committee's activities ultimately resulted in improvements to the audit committee's functions and operations. (These should be reviewed not only to see if the same improvements are still relevant but also to determine what prevented the improvement from occurring in the prior year.)

These are just a few suggestions meant to trigger a meaningful discussion among the committee members and lead to a healthy discussion about the committee's functioning. The audit committee might also consider asking the independent auditor, the governing board, and management for any suggestions they might have for improving the operations of the audit committee. The committee can then assess whether any of these recommendations merit its attention.

Performing an annual evaluation of the audit committee's function is not, however, the best practice to be learned from this section. Rather, the best practice is to set up an action plan to address any shortcomings or areas for improvement that come to light as a result of this annual assessment. With that in mind, the results of the annual assessment process should be documented, along with a list of action items that include who is responsible for acting on those action items.

BEST PRACTICE

The audit committee should prepare an annual report of its activities and use the report to perform a review and evaluation of its activities for the preceding year. An action plan of improvements needed to the audit committee's activities should be compiled by the committee to make sure those improvements are implemented.

ABILITY TO HIRE OUTSIDE COUNSEL AND OTHER ADVISORS

One of the important requirements of the Sarbanes-Oxley Act is to give audit committees of public companies the ability to hire their own legal counsel or other advisors to assist them in performing their functions. The term "other advisors" is obviously broad, but an example of an advisor that comes to mind immediately is that of an actuary who can assist the committee in matters such as pensions, postemployment health care benefits, claims liabilities, and similar types of obligations. There is no requirement that the audit committee must engage any of these outside parties; rather, the requirement is that they be given the ability and authority to do so, if they so desire.

On the face of it, it would seem that granting a not-for-profit organization's audit committee the same capability and authority would constitute a best practice for these committees. My opinion is that this requirement is more important from the perception point of view, as opposed to resulting in numerous not-for-profit organization audit committees going out and hiring a multitude of advisors. The perception resulting from this capability is that the audit committee has access to independent sources of information and counsel outside of what is—forgive the term—"spoon-fed" them by management. Let's face it, much of the information received by the audit committee is coming through the not-for-profit organization's management. While the audit committee can benefit from information provided by the not-for-profit organization's independent auditor, many auditors are reluctant to provide information beyond what is required in the professional standards, particularly if this information is at odds with management's own beliefs and assertions to the audit committee. Authorizing the audit committee to hire its own independent counsel and other advisors not only gives the committee the authority to challenge management's representations to the committee with its own information, it also sends a message to management that they should be objective in providing the committee with the information they need to make intelligent judgments about the accounting and financial reporting practices of the not-for-profit organization.

The other benefit derived from giving the audit committee this capability is that the committee can obtain legal advice when it deems necessary. So far we have discussed many of the responsibilities of audit committees and their members (and many more responsibilities are to come), and there may be situations where audit committee members desire or need to make sure that they are complying with federal and state laws, regulations, and other requirements. These requirements may not specifically be directed to audit committees, but keep in mind that the audit committee is performing functions on behalf of the governing board, and there are a number of governance issues related to governing boards as a whole, particularly at the state level. Having the ability to hire legal counsel to address any difficult area encountered is important for audit committee members to have, so that they be assured that they are fulfilling their tasks and responsibilities within the letter and spirit of the law.

BEST PRACTICE

The audit committee should be authorized to hire outside counsel and other advisors to assist it in discharging its responsibilities.

CONFLICTS-OF-INTEREST STATEMENTS

Earlier in this chapter we discussed the extent of independence that should be required of audit committee members, and the importance of ensuring that committee members are free of conflicts of interest. The best way to ensure that the audit committee members understand what is required of them, and to enable the not-for-profit organization to document its procedures for ensuring that the committee members do not have conflicts of interest, is to have the committee members submit conflicts-of-interest statements to the not-for-profit organization on an annual basis. These statements may be required by the not-for-profit organization from all governing board members; if so, the requirements for audit committee members who are also governing board members can be coordinated. The forms are likely to be the same, so there is no reason to have audit committee members complete two identical forms.

Exhibit 2.2 provides a sample of a conflicts-of-interest statement that can be used as a basis for developing one relevant to the particular not-for-profit organization. Note that the statement requires the audit committee member to confirm

Exhibit 2.2   Sample Conflicts-of-Interest Disclosure Statement

This disclosure statement is being prepared to comply with the XYZ Not-for-Profit Organization's Conflict-of-Interest Policy. All answers given are to the best of my knowledge and belief. This statement is being completed to disclose conflicts of interest and potential conflicts of interest of myself, as well as such conflicts and potential conflicts that arise because of related parties and affiliated organizations.

For purposes of these disclosures, I understand an affiliated organization to be one that I have significance over or which has significant influence over me. A "related party" means my spouse, spousal equivalent, parent, dependent or nondependent child, sibling, employer, employee, or business partner, or equivalent. Related parties also include any person whose relationship with myself could in any way affect my judgment.

1. Name _____

2. I confirm that I have read and will abide by the XYZ Not-for-Profit Organization's Conflicts-of-Interest Policy.

3. Have you or any related parties or affiliated organization provided compensated services or property to the XYZ Not-for-Profit Organization or any affiliated organization (hereafter collectively referred to as the "organization")?

    ___ Yes   ___ No

    If yes, please provide the details below.

4. Do you or any related party or affiliated organization currently have, have had in the past, or will have any direct or indirect interest in any business transactions to which the Organization was or is a party?

    ___ Yes   ___ No

    If yes, please provide the details below.

5. Have you or any related party or affiliated organization purchased services or property from the Organization during the past year?

    ___ Yes   ___ No

    If yes, please provide the details below.

6. Have you or any related party or affiliated organization been indebted to the Organization at any time during the past year?

    ___ Yes   ___ No

    If yes, please provide the details below.

7. Have you or any related party or affiliated organization earned or received any personal benefit as a result of your relationship with the Organization?

    ___ Yes   ___ No

    If yes, please provide the details below.

Exhibit 2.2   Sample Conflicts-of-Interest Disclosure Statement (continued)

8. Have you or any related party or affiliated organization been involved during the past year with any legal proceedings involving the Organization?

___ Yes   ___ No

If yes, please provide the details below.

9. Please describe below any other transactions, events, arrangements, contracts, or other situations involving yourself or any related parties or affiliated organizations that should be examined to determine whether there is a potential conflict of interest.

___ Situation describe below   ___ None

I confirm that to the best of my knowledge and belief the responses provided in this disclosure statement are complete and accurate.

Signature	Date

---

that he or she has read the not-for-profit organization's conflicts-of-interest policy. Not-for-profit organizations should adopt a policy regarding conflicts of interest that should cover both employees of the organization and members of the governing board, including the audit committee members. Details of this type of policy are beyond the scope of this book, but generally speaking, these policies are meant to ensure that employees and governing board members (and organizations with which they are affiliated or related to) cannot benefit from their functions within the not-for-profit organization. For example, assume that an audit committee member of a not-for-profit organization owns a stationery supply store, and the not-for-profit organization buys all of its office supplies from that store. This example would violate most organization's conflicts-of-interest policies. On the other hand, the fact that an audit committee member owns 100 shares of stock in Staples, and the not-for-profit organization buys some of its supplies from Staples, would not likely be a considered a conflict of interest for the audit committee member.

In using the basic conflicts-of-interest statements in Exhibit 2.2 as a guide, the two examples above should indicate of how a yes answer to a question regarding business dealings with the not-for-profit organization might automatically indicate a conflict of interest. The purpose of the conflicts-of-interest statement is to identify potential relationships that might constitute conflicts of interests that can be evaluated by management, the governing board, and, perhaps, legal counsel.

BEST PRACTICE

Require all audit committee members to complete annually a conflicts-of-interest statement so that any potential conflicts of interest for that committee member can be evaluated and resolved.

SUMMARY

This chapter has provided many of the details to consider when establishing an audit committee for a not-for-profit organization and drafting the audit committee's charter and/or bylaws. The subsequent chapters of this book will cover the main areas in which the committee will function and will build on the committee foundation established in this chapter.

Chapter 3

Responsibilities of Internal Control over Financial Reporting

This chapter will provide information to audit committee members as to what their responsibilities are regarding a not-for-profit organization's internal control over financial reporting. Audit committees of not-for-profit organizations that want to employ best practices in fulfilling their responsibilities must be aware that internal control is an integral part of the financial reporting process. It's relatively easy to understand that internal control is a good thing, but audit committee members need to have more than a superficial understanding about these controls. It is also critically important that audit committee members understand the risk of management override of internal control. Best practices require that audit committee members have sufficient knowledge to understand what internal control is, their responsibilities relating to internal control, and the various options that a not-for-profit organization has in terms of ensuring that its internal control process is effectively designed and operating as prescribed.

To accomplish these goals, this chapter is divided into the following sections:

- Internal control basics
- Risks of management override of internal control
- Relationship of internal control to financial reporting
- Options for reporting by management and independent auditors on internal control

After reviewing these areas, audit committee members should feel more confident that they understand their responsibilities relating to internal control, hence should be able to work jointly with the not-for-profit organization's management and the external auditors in ensuring that the organization's internal control is appropriate and effective.

INTERNAL CONTROL BASICS

"Internal control" is a commonly used phrase, so audit committee members might have a general idea what is meant by it. However, a general level of understanding is simply not enough for an audit committee to effectively fulfill his or her responsibilities to the audit committee and the not-for-profit organization. Fortunately, there has been a lot of attention paid to defining internal control recently. This is due to certain requirements of the Sarbanes-Oxley Act relating to requirements that managements of public companies must assess internal control over financial reporting and make assertions as to its effectiveness; similarly, independent auditors must attest to whether those assertions are valid, based upon the auditor's tests of internal control. Whether not-for-profit organizations desire to self-impose these requirements is the topic addressed in the section of this chapter dealing with the various options available relating to internal control.

This chapter's discussions of internal control are based upon a document titled "Internal Control—Integrated Framework," published by the Committee of Sponsoring Organizations of the Treadway Commission (COSO). There always seems to be a great deal of confusion as to what COSO is, so Exhibit 3.1 seeks to clear up some of this. There are two important reasons why the background material on internal control in this chapter is based on this document (which hereafter is referred to as the "control framework"):

1. Independent auditors performing audits of financial statements must comply with generally accepted auditing standards (GAAP), which include requirements as to consideration of internal control. Those auditing standards use the COSO control framework in setting the audit requirements for auditors as to internal control. (The specific auditing standard is the Statement on Auditing Standards No. 78, "Consideration of Internal Control in a Financial Statement Audit—an Amendment to Statement on Auditing Standards No. 55" (SAS-78), which is also a source for the material presented in this chapter.

2. The Sarbanes-Oxley Act requirements just described above require that management make its assertions about internal control using an integrated framework of internal control that is generally known and accepted. While the act doesn't specifically state that the COSO control framework be used, in practice, this is the internal control framework in wide use among public companies and their auditors to meet the Sarbanes-Oxley Act requirements, giving even more credibility to this control framework.

The control framework defines internal control as follows:

Internal control is a process, effected by an entity's board of directors, management, and other personnel, designed to provide reasonable assurance regarding the achievement of objectives in the following categories:

Reliability of financial reporting

Compliance with applicable laws and regulations

Effectiveness and efficiency of operations

Let's look at these objectives, from the more relevant to the less relevant.

Exhibit 3.1   What Is the COSO?

The Committee of Sponsoring Organizations of the Treadway Commission is a private sector organization whose mission is to improve the quality of financial reporting through business ethics, effective internal controls, and corporate governance. It is usually referred to either as COSO or the Treadway Commission. It was originally formed in 1985 to sponsor the National Commission on Fraudulent Financial Reporting, an independent private initiative that studied factors that could lead to financial reporting.

The "sponsoring" organizations are five separate professional groups:

- American Accounting Association
- American Institute of Certified Public Accountants
- Financial Executives Institute
- Institute of Internal Auditors
- Institute of Management Accountants

The "Treadway Commission" part of the name refers to James C. Treadway, Jr., who served as the chairman of the National Commission just described. At the time he served as chairman, he was the general counsel of Paine Webber Incorporated. He was also a former commissioner of the United States Securities Exchange Commission.

In addition to "Internal Control—Integrated Framework," COSO has just recently published "Enterprise Risk Management—Integrated Framework," which provides a basis for assessing risks that affect entire enterprises. This framework is much broader than that of the internal control.

Of note for not-for-profit organizations that tend to be much smaller in size than large publicly traded companies, COSO has recently initiated a project titled "Implementing the COSO Control Framework in Smaller Businesses," the outcome of which may be particularly useful to smaller not-for-profit organizations.

Reliability of Financial Reporting

These are the controls that pertain to an entity's objective of preparing financial statements for external purposes, statements that are fairly presented and conform to generally accepted accounting principles (GAAP). Most not-for-profit organizations produce internal financial reports on an interim basis, such as monthly or quarterly, and frequently these interim reports provide budget-to-actual information for the period, as well as year-to-date. In order for management and the governing board to make informed judgments during the course of the fiscal year, these interim reports also must be prepared in accordance with whatever basis the users of the reports desire. While the audit committee's interest is primarily with the externally issued GAAP-based financial statements, reliability of internal financial information should also be an objective of an internal control system.

Included within the financial reporting objective (and to some extent the effectiveness and efficiency of the operations objective) is the safeguard of assets. These internal controls would be designed to prevent the unauthorized acquisition, use, or disposition of the not-for-profit organization's assets. To distinguish between the financial reporting and operational objectives, consider these two examples. First, there should be internal controls to ensure that cash received by the organization is promptly deposited in an organization's bank account and correctly recorded in the accounting system—a financial reporting objective. Second, the organization should also have controls to verify that its organization-owned vehicles are not used for employees' personal purposes—an operational objective.

Compliance with Applicable Laws and Regulations

While complying with all laws and regulations should be an objective of an internal control system, the audit committee will be primarily interested in those controls that prevent or detect situations where noncompliance with laws and regulations could have a direct impact on the financial statements. For example, if a not-for-profit organization did not comply with some significant requirement of the Internal Revenue Service, and thereby lost its tax-exempt status, there would be serious repercussions on the financial statements, such as the need to record an income tax expense provision, and perhaps even require disclosures about the organization's capability to continue as a going concern. A more common example would involve compliance with various governmental and nongovernmental grants and contracts, where noncompliance might require refund of the grant dollars relating to the area of noncompliance.

Effectiveness and Efficiency of Operations

Although this is an excellent objective for an internal control system, it is probably the most far removed from the audit committee's responsibilities as to internal control. However, controls that prevent overspending in the areas of administration and fund-raising can be viewed as important in maintaining a not-for-profit organization's ability to continue to obtain contributions from donors, which are the lifeline for many not-for-profits operating income.

Keeping these objectives in mind, the next step is to understand what makes up the internal controls that should be in place to meet these objectives. The control framework identifies five interrelated components that comprise internal control. These are:

1. Control environment
2. Risk assessment
3. Control activities
4. Information and communication
5. Monitoring

The following pages describe each of these components of internal control, particularly as they relate to the financial reporting objective, which is of primary importance to the audit committee members. These are the same components and considerations that independent auditors use in accordance with SAS-78 in performing audits of financial statements.

Control Environment. The somewhat overused phrase to describe an organization's control environment is the "tone at the top." It is the internal control component that is based on the consciousness of control among an organization's employees, particularly its management. It is fundamental to all other components of internal control because it provides the discipline and structure upon which all other controls are based. The following factors, which are part of the control environment, will make the concept of the control environment a little less esoteric. Here is a quick example to keep in mind when reading through these factors. Organizations A and B both have an internal control (we'll learn later that this is part of the control activities component) that a check request must be signed by both the preparer of the request and by an individual authorized to approve check requests before a check is prepared. Here are two extremes of control environments:

- Organization A's check preparer allows a check to be issued without the approver's signature on the check request. The organization's management learns of the violation of the internal control and terminates the employment of the check preparer.

- Organization B's check preparer routinely allows checks to be issued without the signature of the check request approver. He or she knows that a day or two before the independent auditor comes in for the annual audit, the approver will sit down with all of the check requests for the year and sign them. Management is aware of this control violation, but looks the other way because everyone at the organization is overworked and there is just no time to follow the procedures during the year.

With this example in mind, consider the following factors that comprise the control environment internal control component.

Integrity and Ethical Values The effectiveness of controls depends on the integrity and ethical values of the people who create, administer, and monitor them. Integrity and ethical behavior are the products of an organization's ethical and behavioral standards: specifically, how they are communicated and how they are reinforced in practice. Included in this factor are management's actions to remove or reduce incentives and temptations that might prompt personnel to engage in dishonest, illegal, or unethical acts. This factor also includes communication of the organization's values and behavioral standards to personnel through policy statements and codes of conduct, as well as by example.

Commitment to Competence Competence in this case means the knowledge and skills necessary to accomplish an employee's job. Management must appropriately match the tasks that individuals are assigned with the skills sets possessed by these individuals. For example, assigning a new college graduate to run an organization's interest rate swap program may not be the best idea to maintain good controls.

Board of Directors and Audit Committee Participation Yes, the governing board and the audit committee comprise part of the control environment of the not-for-profit organization. Effective attributes (many of which have already been discussed in detail in Chapter 2) include independence from management, experience and stature of members, extent of involvement and scrutiny of activities, appropriateness of actions, the degree to which difficult questions are raised and pursued with management, and the interaction with external and internal auditors.

Management Philosophy and Operating Style   Characteristics of a management's philosophy and operating style include their approach to taking and monitoring business risks, attitudes and actions toward financial reporting, as well as attitudes toward information processing and accounting functions and personnel. Audit committee members can learn a lot about management's operating style by encouraging frequent and open communications with members of management, as well as from receiving input from others, such as the independent auditors.

Organizational Structure   The not-for-profit organization's organizational structure provides the framework within which activities are planned, executed, controlled, and monitored. Key areas of authority and responsibility need to be considered along with appropriate lines of reporting. The appropriateness of the organizational structure is dependent on the organization's size and the nature of its activities.

Assignment of Authority and Responsibility   This factor includes how authority and responsibility for operating activities are assigned, along with how reporting relationships and authorization hierarchies are established. It also includes policies relating to appropriate business practices, knowledge and experience of key personnel, and resources provided for carrying out duties. This control environment factor also relates to policies and communications directed at ensuring that all personnel understand the organization's objectives.

Human Resource Policies and Practices   This factor relates to hiring, orientation, training, evaluating, counseling, promoting, compensating, and remedial actions. Human resources policies and procedures can demonstrate whether an organization is committed to hiring competent and trustworthy people. Adequate training and promotion of the most competent people are important contributors to a healthy control environment in a not-for-profit organization.

   In considering these factors about the control environment of a not-for-profit organization, there are a few of things that an audit committee member should keep in mind:

- When a not-for-profit organization has more than one office location, the control environment within each office may be different. For national organizations that work through local offices or branches, the control environment at the branch level may be very different from that found at the home office. This is particularly important when financial activities are decentralized and branches are entering into and recording financial transactions at their individual levels.

- Management is likely to present the control environment in the best light possible. It may take some specific, probing questions before a clearer understanding of the control environment is learned.

- An emphasis of substance over form must be maintained. In the control environment example of organizations A and B described earlier, would anyone be surprised if organization B had adopted a well written, thoughtful code of conduct that it simply chose to ignore on a daily basis?

BEST PRACTICE

Audit committee members should have an understanding of the control environment in which the not-for-profit organization operates. This understanding extends beyond that of simply knowing how accounting transactions are processed.

Risk Assessment. Risk assessment is the next component of the internal control framework that needs to be understood. Risk assessment for financial reporting purposes comprises a not-for-profit organization's identification, analysis, and management of risks relative to the preparation of financial statements.

The first step in risk assessment is to identify risks. It's difficult, maybe impossible, to develop a good system of internal control if it is unclear what risks the system is trying to mitigate. Risks for financial reporting include external and internal events and circumstances that may occur that would adversely affect an organization's ability to initiate, record, process, and report financial data consistent with the assertions of management in the financial statements. For example, there is a risk that all of the transactions that an organization enters into are not captured by its accounting system. There is also a risk that the accounting system reflects transactions that did not actually occur. There is a third risk that transactions that did occur and were captured by the accounting system were captured in the wrong amounts. It's not likely that a not-for-profit organization considered all of the financial reporting risks to which it is subject at the same time. Many times, as new systems and processes are implemented, the risks relative to these new systems or processes are considered at the time of implementation. In other words, identifying risks is often an ongoing process rather than an annual event.

The second step in the risk-assessment process is to perform an analysis of the risks. Risks need to be analyzed for the various different balance sheet and operating statement accounts, for the classes of transactions in which the organization participates, as well as for the adequacy of disclosures in the financial statements. For the various risks that have been identified, management considers their significance, the likelihood of their occurrence, and how they should be managed. For example, let's say that a not-for-profit organization identifies as a risk that transactions that occur may not be entered into its accounting system. This same risk is different for various types of accounts and transactions. For example, the risk that cash donations to the organization are not captured and reported on the financial statements is different from the risk that a sale of a building that the not-for-profit organization owns would not be recorded in the financial statements.

The third step in the risk assessment process is for management to initiate plans, programs, or actions that address the risks that have been identified and analyzed. The more detailed controls that result from management's actions will be discussed at greater length in the control activities section that follows.

The internal control framework notes that risks can change over time, and lists a number of factors that may cause changes to the risks that are faced by an organization. These factors include:

- Changes in operating environment (including changes to the regulatory environment)
- New personnel
- New or revamped information systems
- Rapid growth
- New technology
- New business models, products, or activities
- Corporate restructurings
- Expanded foreign operations
- New accounting pronouncements

Even though some of these factors appear more to use terminology more relevant to business operations, they can apply equally to not-for-profit organizations. For example, while many not-for-profit organizations do not offer new "products," the introduction of a new category of program activities, or perhaps accepting a federal award for the first time, are changes that can certainly affect the risks related to financial reporting.

BEST PRACTICE

The audit committee members should be briefed by management as to how they assess risks faced by the organization related to financial reporting.

Control Activities. Control activities are likely to be what many think of when internal control comes to mind. A second, independent party review of an accounting entry is an example of this type of component of internal control. However, the internal control framework's definition of control activities is broader. Control activities relevant to internal control over financial reporting are categorized as follows:

- *Performance reviews.* No, these are not personnel performance reviews. They are comparisons of actual reported amounts with other measures to see if the actual reported amounts make sense. For example, actual results may be compared to budgeted amounts or to the prior year's results. Particularly for comparisons with the prior year's results, simply because the numbers are the same or similar doesn't mean that the actual amounts are properly stated. There may have been reasons why the current year's amounts should be significantly different from the prior year's amounts. The essence of this control is that the comparisons made result in a careful analysis of differences, or lack of differences, to give management a better understanding of the reported amounts. These comparisons also ideally relate to operating data as well. For example, payroll expense during a year is influenced by several factors, including the number of employees on payroll. Factoring in operating data, such as number of employees, provides yet a higher level of control over the amounts reported in the financial statements.

- *Information processing.* Control activities relating to information processing are categorized into two types of controls: general controls and application controls.

  - General controls include controls over the data center and network operations, system software acquisition and maintenance, access security and application system acquisition, development, and maintenance. Examples include controls over any changes made to computer programs used in operations, controls that restrict access to programs or data, controls over implementation of new releases of packaged software, and software controls that restrict access to and monitor the use of systems utility programs.

  - Application controls are those that apply to the running of individual programs or applications. They help ensure that transactions that occur are authorized and completely and accurately recorded and processed. For example, when processing changes to receivables, does the beginning receivable balance, plus new receivables, less cash collections applied to receivables tie in to the ending receivable balance?

- *Physical controls.* Physical controls refer literally to those controls over the physical security of assets, including safeguards such as secured facilities, limitations on access to assets and records, authorization for access to computer programs and data files, as well as the periodic counting of assets compared with amounts recorded on control records. Hence, physical controls encompass not only those assets that are tangible (such as a fence around an inventory storage location) but also those that are less tangible (such as computer software and data files.) In addition, the physical controls involve more than those that take a physical form (such as the safe where the petty cash box is stored at night); they also can take the form of a process (taking a physical inventory of the goods for sale at the museum gift shop and comparing the counts to the inventory records maintained by the gift shop.)

- *Segregation of duties.* This is a common phrase heard in discussions about internal control and is an important factor in the control activities component of internal control. Segregation of duties is based on the concept that it is much more difficult to prevent or detect an error when the responsibilities for authorizing transactions, recording transactions, and maintaining the custody of assets are handled by different individuals. It is intended to reduce the opportunities for any one person to be in a position to both perpetrate and conceal errors or fraud in the normal course of his or her duties. In the case of fraudulent activities, perpetuating the fraud where there is segregation of duties would require two people to be in on the fraud, which is much more difficult (although certainly not impossible) than if one person were able to act individually. On the other hand, even when there is no deliberate intention to commit a fraudulent act, segregation of duties can be useful to provide that "other set of eyes" that can be useful in preventing or detecting unintentional errors.

BEST PRACTICE

The audit committee should ask management about the not-for-profit organization's strategies for maintaining effective control activities.

Information and Communication.   This component of internal control has two aspects: information systems and communications. They will be examined in turn.

Information Systems   Information systems are those that consist of infrastructure (such as computer hardware and related components), software, people, procedures, and data. Note that the term "information systems" in this context is not synonymous with information technology. An information system can be mostly manual, in which case the system will have little in the way of computer infrastructure and software, but would be considered an information system nonetheless. That said, many information systems do make extensive use of information technology.

The information system relative to internal controls over financial reporting, which includes the accounting system, consists of the procedures (both automated and manual) and records established to initiate, record, process, and report the not-for-profit organization's transactions, as well as to maintain accountability for assets, liabilities and net assets. Processing in this context includes functions such as editing, validating, calculation, measurement, valuation, summarization, and reconciliation. The quality of system-generated information affects management's ability to make appropriate decisions, as well as the ability of the organization to prepare reliable financial statements.

An information system encompasses methods and records that do the following:

- Identify and record all valid transactions.
- Describe transactions on a timely basis and in sufficient detail to permit proper classification of transactions for financial reporting.

- Measure the value of transactions in a manner that permits recording their proper monetary value in the financial statements.
- Determine the time period in which transactions occur so that they can be recorded in the proper accounting period.
- Present properly the transactions and related disclosures in the organization's financial statements.

Again, the information system that is designed to accomplish these requirements can be either manual or automated. The same system may also have both manual and automated features.

Communications   The purpose of effective communications is to make sure that the individuals who have roles and responsibilities in internal control related to financial reporting understand precisely what their role entails. Communication includes the extent to which personnel recognize how their activities in the financial reporting information system relate to the work of others, and the means of reporting exceptions to an appropriate higher level within the organization. In other words, people involved in the internal control over financial reporting have to know that their roles are important and need to be taken seriously. In addition, they must be aware that any problems or exceptions with the controls that they are performing need to be reported and addressed to an appropriately higher level within the organization. This includes making sure that they understand that their immediate supervisor doesn't have the right to ignore exceptions or problems that are called to his or her attention.

There are many different forms of communications: written, oral, and electronic, as well as by actions of management. Some of the common forms of written communications include policy manuals, accounting manuals, financial reporting manuals, and various forms of instruction memoranda. One problem often encountered with written communications is keeping the information up to date. For example, if a not-for-profit organization's accounting manual hasn't been updated in the 10 years since it was written, chances are that it is not providing an effective means of communication.

BEST PRACTICE

The audit committee should have a basic understanding of the important systems on which the organization's financial reporting process is based. Challenging management as to the how complete and current its communications are with personnel is also an appropriate action.

Monitoring.   Some might think that monitoring is synonymous with internal control, but in this context its meaning is more specific. Monitoring is the process that assesses the quality of internal control performance over time. Management should not design and implement an internal control system and then fail to review whether the system is effective. Rather, it should assess both the design and actual operation of the system on a timely basis and take any corrective actions that are necessary.

How does management monitor the effectiveness of the organization's internal control system? The most direct answer involves incorporating steps in the not-for-profit organization's annual financial reporting processes to provide the means by which individuals directly and indirectly involved in the internal control over financial reporting can identify necessary changes and recommend their implementation. If the not-for-profit organization has an internal audit function (this is discussed in a later chapter of this book), this is a classic way of management: The governing board and the audit committee obtain feedback about how well the financial reporting (and other) controls in the organization are designed and whether they are operating as specified.

In addition to these effective monitoring mechanisms, management should pay attention to other types of information that it obtains from less formal channels of communication, which might provide feedback as to how well the not-for-profit organization's internal controls are working. For example:

- Do suppliers return checks to the not-for-profit organization stating that their invoice was already paid?
- Do suppliers complain that they have not been paid for abnormally long periods of time (assuming the organization does not have cash flow difficulties and is paying its bill regularly)?
- Do donors complain that they do not receive acknowledgment letters (or receive letters for the wrong amount) for contributions that they have made to the organization?
- Do employees find many errors on their paychecks or on the W-2 forms that they receive from the organization at the end of the year?
- Do audits conducted by or on behalf of a funding source (such as single audits performed for recipients of federal awards programs) report internal control or compliance findings?

These are just a few examples of different types of items that might give management some circumstantial evidence that internal controls may not be properly designed or are not operating properly.

BEST PRACTICE

The audit committee should request management to inform it about how it monitors the effectiveness of the design and operation of internal controls related to financial reporting.

RISKS OF MANAGEMENT OVERRIDE OF CONTROLS

The preceding discussion of the internal control framework as it relates to financial reporting is designed to familiarize audit committee members with the various types of internal controls that can be used by not-for-profit organizations. The point is to minimize the risk that misstatements of their financial statements occur because the internal controls did not prevent or detect a material error or fraud from occurring. Audit committee members might come away from this brief overview wondering how so many of the financial reporting problems that have come to light in recent years could have occurred, given the many mechanism available to provide excellent internal control over financial reporting. The answer is that there is an important, overarching weakness to which virtually all systems of internal control are prey: management override of those controls.

Audit committee members may be familiar with the recent accounting scandals that have afflicted public companies, which at the start of this book were cited as a primary reason for the current interest in improving the functioning of all audit committees, including those of not-for-profit organizations. Upon further examination of many of these scandals, however, the focus of the investigations and legal proceedings was not on the accounts payable supervisor who forgot to sign off on a disbursement request before a check to a vendor was issued. Rather, in many of those cases, management, allegedly, caused large accounting entries to be recorded that were based upon, at best, questionable and, at worst, fraudulent, analyses of the actual facts and circumstances. In other words, they deliberately caused entries to be made to distort earnings, hide debt, or for some other motive that would not have been recorded in the ordinary conduct of business. In other words, they overrode or bypassed the internal control system.

Picture this scenario: The president and chief financial officer of a large publicly traded company know that the company's financial results will miss the community of stock analysts' earnings expectations for the current quarter by 5 cents per share, or $50 million. Not wanting to see a stock decline, the chief financial officer instructs the company's controller to have an accounting entry recorded to reduce the company's allowance for uncollectible receivables by $50 million, which, forgetting about tax implications for the moment, will increase earnings by this amount, enabling the company to meet the stock analysts' financial projections. The controller then tells the accounting manager to record this entry, explaining that the company expects to implement aggressive new collection techniques that will result in fewer uncollectible accounts receivable. The accounting manager tells the accountant in charge of this account to prepare the entry, provides the same explanation, and notes that the entry is coming from the chief financial officer. Now this accountant has spent the last month crunching numbers that would result in the normal adjustment to the allowance for uncollectible receivables. His or her calculations were already approved by the accounting manager and recorded in the accounting system. Nevertheless, to ensure job security, the accountant prepares the new accounting entry, the accounting manager approves it, it is entered into the accounting system, and the company's earnings target is met.

This example is one of classic management override. The internal control system worked well, up to the point where senior management overrode the system. Note that from an internal control point of view, the control procedures were followed, in that the bogus accounting entry went through the appropriate approval channels. The only thing that went wrong was that management chose to make up the numbers. It would take an awful lot for the accountant and the accounting manager to stand up to the edicts of the chief financial officer. The controller would presumably be in a better position to dispute the entry, but he or she may be in a high enough position where a decline in stock price might affect an anticipated bonus payment or devalue some of the individual's stock options.

Not-for-profit organizations have different pressures on financial reporting, although the management override process would work the same. Instead of earnings targets, assume that an executive director and chief financial officer of a not-for-profit organization instructed the same entry to be recorded because they didn't want the organization to exceed its budget for the quarter. Or perhaps administrative expenses of the organization appeared to be too high, so an accounting entry was ordered that moved costs from administrative activities to program activities. The motives or types of entries may be slightly different, but the risks resulting from a management override of internal control over financial reporting are just as high at a not-for-profit organization as they are at public companies.

Audit committee members must address the issue of management override of internal control over financial reporting for several reasons. One is that it simply doesn't make sense to spend time and effort learning and implementing an organization's internal control over financial reporting if those controls can be easily overrode by management. A second reason is that it is difficult for personnel below the senior management level of an organization to do something about management override without feeling that they are risking their jobs. Because management is doing the override, that leaves the governing board and the audit committee with the best chance of ensuring that procedures and processes are in place to minimize, to an acceptable level, the risk that management may override controls.

The issue is of such importance that the American Institute of Certified Public Accountants (AICPA) issued a document meant to facilitate an audit committee's consideration of the risk of management override. The document, titled "Management Override of Internal Controls: The Achilles' Heel of Fraud Prevention" (hereafter, AICPA Task Force Report) presents the views of the AICPA's Antifraud Programs and Controls Task Force, and includes as its specific purpose to offer guidance to audit committees in addressing the risk of fraud through management override of internal control over financial reporting. As of this writing, the document is available for download free of charge from the AICPA's Web site, www.aicpa.org.

The AICPA Task Force Report lists three ways management might override controls to misstate the financial statements:

1. Record fictitious business events or transactions or change the timing of recognition of legitimate transactions, particularly those recorded close to the end of an accounting period.

2. Establish or reverse reserves to manipulate results, including intentionally biasing assumptions and judgments used to estimate account balances.

3. Alter records and terms related to significant or unusual transactions.

The example of management override just presented most closely matches the second method here, where a reserve is reversed based upon a bias in the method used to estimate the reserve.

The seriousness with which the AICPA Task Force Report describes the audit committee's responsibilities as to management override of controls is clear from this excerpt:

> The board of directors and the audit committee are responsible for overseeing the actions of management. Corporate directors can no longer argue that they acted diligently in carrying out their responsibilities if they failed to design a strong audit committee charter and timely perform all the functions specified therein. With respect to audit committee members, this included the duty to inquire into the adequacy of their corporation's internal controls, both in theory and in practice, and to take actions, such as those described in this document, to minimize the possibility that internal controls are overridden by management, thereby resulting in undetected fraud.

These are strong words to include in a document such as this and, although one can argue that the focus of the document (although not explicitly stated) is to help audit committees of public companies, not-for-profit organizations also should take the recommendations of the AICPA Task Force Report seriously. These recommendations, which not-for-profits should incorporate in their operating procedures, are summarized in the following practices.

BEST PRACTICE

The audit committee should address the risk of management override of internal control, which includes incorporating the recommendations of the AICPA Task Force Report into the audit committee's standard procedures.

The following sections summarize the basic recommendations of the AICPA Task Force Report, which an audit committee should act upon to help fulfill its obligations relating to the risk of management override of internal control over financial reporting:

Maintain Skepticism

Independent auditors are familiar with the concept of skepticism in performing an audit. Skepticism acknowledges that fraud risks (including the risk of management override) exist in every organization. This doesn't mean that the committee members should disbelieve everything that management tells them; it does mean that audit committee members shouldn't assume that management is always telling the truth. Audit committee members need to be alert to the fraud risk factors (discussed in a separate chapter) and be willing to ask tough, sometimes embarrassing, questions. Audit committee members are also encouraged to hold open and candid discussions about the risks of management override and consider what-if scenarios related to the possibilities of fraud at the organization.

Strengthen Committee Understanding of the Business

Audit committee members are encouraged to gain a solid knowledge of the industry in which the organization operates. Organization and industry knowledge is critical for determining whether the organization's financial reporting is sufficient for its readers. This knowledge also helps audit committee members anticipate fraud risk factors that might be prevalent in the industry in which the organization operates. It's not really enough to categorize all not-for-profit organizations as being in the not-for-profit industry. As stated in previous chapters, not-for-profit colleges and universities are far different from, say, hospitals, which are far different from social service organizations, and so on. In order to have a reasonable chance of identifying fraud risk factors in advance of a breakdown in financial reporting, the audit committee members need knowledge of the specific organization and the niche in which it operates if they are to identify the key drivers of the key performance indicators.

In addition to understanding the not-for-profit organization's business and industry, AICPA Task Force Report lists the following as important matters for the audit committee to understand or take action on:

- Understand what might threaten management's ability to accomplish its objectives and strategies. These factors might include competition for contracts, grants, or donations with other organizations; loss of a major contract or donor; or regulatory issues.

- Understand the reporting environment in which those responsible for financial reporting operate. This may include the relationship of the financial reporting personnel with other functional areas of the not-for-profit organization, as well as unrealistic performance expectations that serve as a catalyst for financial statement fraud.

- Understand the process for developing, reviewing, and revising budget, in conjunctions with the organization's "budgeting mentality." The budgeting mentality is important in considering budgetary expectations that are set. For example, a budget that is intended to be used as an incentive for various areas to reach their greatest potential (such as an increase in contribution revenue or a decrease in administrative expenses) can create pressures to falsify reported results.

- Finally, understand how executive compensation is tied to financial performance. True, there are fewer obvious ties in not-for-profit organizations than in commercial organizations, but they may still exist. For example, the director of development who is looking for a large salary increase because of successes in fund-raising efforts may have the incentive to overstate contributions receivable from donors, or try to make conditional donor pledges appear as if they are unconditional, resulting in contribution revenue being recorded when it shouldn't be.

Brainstorm to Identify Fraud Risks

This suggested action is similar to what members of the audit team of the independent auditor of the financial statements are required to do as part of their audit under the AICPA's auditing standards. Audit committee members can increase their effectiveness in dealing with the potential of management override of internal control by discussing, among themselves, the potential for fraud. This exchange of ideas would include how and where they believe the organization may be susceptible to fraud, what might motivate management to perpetrate fraud, how management might override controls to engage in and conceal fraudulent financial reporting, and how the organization's assets could be misappropriated.

The AICPA Task Force Report recommends that the brainstorming session include consideration of both external and internal factors affecting the organization that might:

- Create incentives or pressures for management and others to committee fraud.
- Provide the opportunity for fraud to be perpetrated.
- Indicate a culture or environment that enables management to rationalize committing fraud.

In addition, audit committee discussions with internal auditors, independent auditors, counsel, the compensation committee, human resources, the compliance officer, and fund-raising and program leaders may provide important input to the brainstorming sessions.

Use the Code of Conduct to Assess Financial Reporting Culture

Although many organizations have a code of conduct, just the existence of such a code is not sufficient to reduce the likelihood of management override of controls. The AICPA Task Force Report suggests that the audit committee be routinely furnished with the results of any surveys of employees regarding corporate behavior and similar information received from external parties. The purpose of this information is to provide more input about the "tone at the top," which was discussed earlier in this chapter. The extent to which management is perceived to be committed to the code of conduct tells the audit committee a great deal about its ability to prevent or detect management override of controls. In addition, the audit committee should evaluate how management communicates information about the code of conduct and motivates employees to comply with the code as a means of obtaining information about the culture and attitudes toward ethical behavior within the organization.

Cultivate a Vigorous Whistleblower Program

A later chapter in this book will prescribe best practices to help audit committees design an effective whistleblower program. A whistleblower program is a mechanism by which employees (or others) can report on unethical (or other unacceptable) conduct by management within the organization. The nature of the program must be such that the complaint reaches a sufficiently high level in the organization to ensure that it is handled properly (i.e., not squashed) and that the individual reporting such behavior is protected from retaliation by those involved.

The AICPA Task Force Report notes that an effective whistleblower program typically incorporates the use of a telephone hotline. It also suggests that to effectively monitor the risk of management override of internal control, the audit committee must automatically and directly receive all complaints involving senior management. These complaints can't be filtered through management or someone else within the organization.

Develop a Broad Information and Feedback Network

The AICPA Task Force Report recommends that the audit committee develop an extensive information network that extends beyond senior management, in order to significantly increase the audit committee's ability to detect management override of internal control. Here are some of the recommendations for others within and outside the organization with whom the audit committee should communicate to obtain feedback on the potential for management override of internal control:

• *Communications with internal auditors.* The audit committee's relationship with the internal audit function will be discussed later in this book. For our purposes here, the overriding point made in the AICPA Task Force Report is that the internal audit department should understand that its responsibilities are primarily to the audit committee. While this concept may need some modification to function effectively in the not-for-profit organization environment, it's sufficient at this point to note that a strong audit committee function may also include the audit committee's oversight of the internal audit department's budget approval process and its policies regarding hiring, evaluation, training, and termination of internal audit staff.

  Executive sessions with the head of the internal audit function at every audit committee meeting are recommended by the AICPA Task Force Report to provide an opportunity to engage in candid discussions about the possible risk of management override of controls and any indications of improper conduct by senior management. A properly directed internal audit staff can serve as, the "eyes and ears" of the audit committee.

- *Communications with independent auditors.* Again, this is a much broader topic, but the AICPA Task Force Report focuses on how these communications can be directed to reduce the risk of management override of internal control. It specifically states that even organizations not subject to the Sarbanes-Oxley Act should consider making the audit committee responsible for the appointment of the independent auditor. In this way, the audit committee can ensure that the independent auditor report directly to the committee. A strong and candid relationship between the audit committee and the independent auditor, including an open dialogue between the two, can provide a useful foundation for the audit committee's assessment of fraud risk, including the risk of management override of internal control.

- *Communications with the compensation committee.* This item will have more limited applicability to not-for-profit organizations; nevertheless, it's important to note that though not-for-profit organization management does not have compensation tied to share price, nor benefits from the receipt of stock options, the organization's financial performance does provide an indication of the effectiveness of management, which ultimately can have an effect on management's compensation. Regardless whether there is a compensation committee or these functions are performed by an executive committee of the governing board, the audit committee should be aware of any ties between the financial performance of the not-for-profit organization and the compensation of management. Note that management may not be judged by a "bottom line" of the organization. Still, the effectiveness of management can often be judged by other financial indicators, such as by the extent to which the not-for-profit organization stays within its budget or the levels of donor contributions that are obtained through fund-raising efforts. These factors can be an incentive for a not-for-profit organization's management to override internal control, and therefore should be understood by the audit committee.

- *Communications with key employees.* As applied to not-for-profit organizations, the AICPA Task Force Report recommendations regarding communications with key employees would result in the audit committee communicating with the general counsel, the human resources department, and compliance, fund-raising, and/or marketing and program leaders. Briefly, the following summarizes the types of information that may be obtained by the audit committee by maintaining effective communications lines with individuals in each of these groups:

  - *General counsel.* The organization's general counsel may be aware of potential violations of laws and regulations, possible violations of the organization's code of conduct, or pressures that management may be experiencing. The general counsel may have information, for example, about pressures to structure significant or unusual transactions designed to achieve financial targets that may create significant incentives to engage in fraud. In addition, the general counsel would have information about major legal risks that the organization might be facing.

- *Human resources.* The audit committee would be interested in the organization's preemployment screening processes, as well as monitoring and employee discipline, which are all part of an organization's effort to prevent fraud. The audit committee would also be interested in the exit interview process and resignation letters with respect to employees in the accounting and finance functions.

- *Compliance officer.* When the function of monitoring the organization's compliance with laws, regulations, donor restrictions and conditions, grant and contract provisions, and other areas is centered in one individual or group, the audit committee should have an open and comfortable relationship with that employee or group. Frequent violations of compliance requirements may indicate a lax or cavalier attitude by management, thus an increased risk of management override of internal control.

- *Fund-raising and/or marketing.* Revenue recognition (i.e., when it is appropriate to record revenue in the financial statements) is a common area for accounting problems, hence there is almost always a risk of fraud in this area. Having open communications with individuals responsible for the revenue areas of a not-for-profit organization can provide the audit committee with information about pressures that may be exerted on these individuals to produce higher recorded revenues, thereby increasing the risk of management override of internal control.

- *Program leaders.* A program in the not-for-profit organization environment can take many different forms, such as a homeless outreach program or a day care program. There may also be various branch locations of organizations, each of which is responsible for certain aspects of the organizations programs. By establishing communication lines with the individuals responsible for these various functions and programs, the audit committee can learn about the types of problems they may be experiencing or the types of pressures that they are under. When these program leaders operate under extreme pressures or incentives, they may be motivated to engage in activities that may include the override of internal control. These program leaders may also be aware of senior management activities to override internal control.

All of the suggestions and recommendations of the AICPA Task Force Report can lead to meaningful actions on the part of the audit committee to address the risk of management override of internal control. While these actions can't eliminate entirely the risk of management's override of internal control, they can serve to reduce this risk to a level acceptable to the audit committee members.

RELATIONSHIP OF INTERNAL CONTROL TO FINANCIAL REPORTING

Now that the basic framework of internal control related to financial reporting has been addressed, along with a discussion of the risks of management's override of those controls, the next logical step for an audit committee member is to understand why he or she should be interested in a not-for-profit organization's internal control over financial reporting. This relationship can be stated very succinctly. The audit committee has an important role in ensuring the propriety of a not-for-profit organization's financial reporting. Internal control over financial reporting is an important element in helping to ensure that the not-for-profit organization's financial reporting is proper and in accordance with generally accepted accounting principles.

Internal controls help ensure that:

- All of the not-for-profit organization's assets, liabilities, revenues, and expenses are captured by its accounting system, at the correct values.
- Only valid assets, liabilities, revenues and expenses are recorded in the not-for-profit organization's accounting system.
- The not-for-profit organization's assets are safeguarded from unauthorized use or disposition.

In other words, internal controls help to provide assurance that the accounting transactions that flow into a not-for-profit organization's financial statements are appropriate. In fact, external auditors, in their audit of financial statements are required to gain an understanding of an organization's internal control system when they are planning their audit and developing an audit strategy. The following summarizes the decisions that independent auditors make when designing an audit strategy for an audit of a not-for-profit organization's financial statements:

- If an organization has well-designed internal controls, the auditor may select certain controls to test, to make sure that they are operating as designed. If they are, the auditor can rely on these controls, thereby reducing the amount of audit testing that they would otherwise have to do on the various accounts that comprise the not-for-profit organization's financial statements. On the other hand, if the audit tests demonstrate that the internal controls are not operating as designed, the auditor cannot rely on these internal controls, which would increase the amount of testing of the various accounts that comprise the not-for-profit organization's financial statements.
- If a not-for-profit organization's internal controls are not well designed, there is no reason for the auditor to test that they are operating as designed. Rather, the auditor would increase the amount of testing of the various accounts that comprise the not-for-profit organization's financial statements, to compensate for the lack of effective controls over financial reporting. This, then, is the same result if the auditor had found that the well designed controls were not operating as designed.

Having gained an understanding of a not-for-profit organization's internal controls for the purpose of auditing the organization's financial statements, the independent auditor may produce a commentary letter on the organization's internal control, commonly referred to as a management letter or report to management. Clearly, this letter is important to audit committee members (and will be discussed in greater detail in a later chapter). For purposes here, it will help to define the different levels of comments that an independent auditor reports, to assist in understanding the letter. Comments can fall into one of three categories:

1. Material weakness in internal control
2. A reportable condition
3. All other comments that are neither material weaknesses nor reportable conditions

A material weakness in internal control is the most serious type of comment. Auditing standards define a material weakness as a condition in which the design or operation of one or more internal control components does not reduce to a relatively low level the risk that misstatements, caused by errors or fraud in amounts that would be material to the financial statements, may occur and not be detected within a timely period by employees in the normal course of performing their defined functions.

A reportable condition is defined in the auditing standards as a matter coming to the auditor's attention that, in his or her judgment, should be communicated to the audit committee because it represents significant deficiencies in the design or operation of internal controls, which could adversely affect the organization's ability to record, process, summarize, and report financial data consistent with the assertions of management in the financial statements.

Notice how both definitions focus on the role of internal controls in accumulating transactions so that financial statements can be prepared. Material weaknesses in internal controls reported by independent auditors are infrequent. Whether the auditor can issue an opinion on the financial statement's compliance with generally accepted accounting principles will depend on whether the auditor can design and perform adequate audit tests to compensate for the material internal control weakness that exists. Many years ago, auditors were required to report to audit committees only material weaknesses in internal controls. Reporting of other comments was optional.

The concept of reportable conditions is an outgrowth of that scenario, where in addressing the general question of which matters should be reported to audit committees, it was concluded that there are other types of internal control deficiencies that, while not rising to the level of material weaknesses, should be required to be reported to audit committees. Hence, the category of control deficiencies called reportable conditions was created. Both material weaknesses (which, by definition, already meet and exceed the requirement to be considered a reportable condition) and reportable conditions are required to be reported to the audit committee by the independent auditor performing an audit of financial statements. Independent auditors are usually able to complete their audit of financial statements and issue their opinion on them even when reportable conditions exist. If this were not the case, it would certainly raise the question of whether the reportable condition should be elevated to the status of a material weakness.

Comments on internal controls that do not rise to the level of reportable conditions do not have to be communicated to the audit committee—although in practice, they usually are reported.

Clearly, audit committee members must be attentive to the communications about internal control received from the independent auditor. An important point to remember is that the audit committee itself is part of an organization's internal control over financial reporting. To fulfill this role, the audit committee must pay careful attention to the all other aspects of an organization's internal control over financial reporting, including those weaknesses reported to it by the organization's independent auditor of its financial statements. This role involves not only considering whether the internal controls are adequate to enable the organization to prepare financial statements in accordance with generally accepted accounting principles, but also to make sure that management is paying careful attention to internal controls and is applying adequate resources to ensure that any existing deficiencies in internal control are being properly addressed.

BEST PRACTICE

The audit committee should have an adequate understanding of the role of internal control in the preparation of financial statements in accordance with generally accepted accounting principles and should address the adequacy of these controls with management and the independent auditor.

OPTIONS FOR REPORTING BY MANAGEMENT AND INDEPENDENT AUDITORS ON INTERNAL CONTROL

The final section of this chapter addresses an issue that some not-for-profit organizations have been struggling with recently relating to internal control. One of the most important provisions of the Sarbanes-Oxley Act that applies to publicly traded companies has to do with internal control. These requirements, commonly referred to as the Section 404 requirements of the Sarbanes-Oxley Act, where they are contained, require management to prepare a written report on internal control that is included in the company's annual report each year. Further, the independent auditor of the financial statements must attest to the assertions that management makes in this written report.

The following discussion is not intended to provide an in-depth analysis of the requirements of Section 404. Nor will the best practice recommended by this section be that all not-for-profit organizations voluntarily comply with Section 404. Rather, this section provides a general understanding of the Section 404 requirements, along with the factors that not-for-profit organizations and their governing boards and audit committees should consider in deciding whether to implement some or all of these requirements.

The rules for implementing Section 404 are the responsibility of the United States Securities and Exchange Commission (SEC). The SEC has issued its "Final

Rule—Management's Reports on Internal Control over Financial Reporting and Certification of Disclosure in Exchange Act Periodic Reports." The Public Company Accounting Oversight Board, which is charged with setting auditing standards for public companies, in March 2004, issued its Auditing Standard No. 2, "An Audit of Internal Control over Financial Reporting Performed in Conjunction with an Audit of Financial Statements" (AS-2). AS-2 tells auditors how they should go about auditing internal control so that they attest to the assertions made by management in its written report.

The SEC's final rules require that a public company's annual report include an internal control report of management, which contains:

- A statement of management's responsibility for establishing and maintaining adequate internal control over financial reporting for the company.
- A statement identifying the framework used by management to conduct the required evaluation of the effectiveness of the company's internal control over financial reporting.
- Management's assessment of the effectiveness of the company's internal control over financial reporting as of the end of the company's most recent fiscal year, including a statement as to whether the company's internal control over financial reporting is effective. The assessment must include disclosure of any "material weaknesses" in the company's internal control over financial reporting. Management is not permitted to conclude that the company's internal control over financial reporting is effective if there are one or more material weaknesses in the company's internal control over financial reporting.
- A statement that the registered public accounting firm that audited the financial statements included in the annual report has issued an attestation report on management's assessment of the registrant's internal control over financial reporting.

The heart of these requirements is contained in the third item, concerning management's assessment of internal control over financial reporting. The last thing that a reader should think about this requirement is that management can issue this assessment based upon its "gut feel" that "our internal controls are terrific" and simply assess the controls to be effective. There are many detailed requirements as to identifying, documenting, and testing internal controls for effectiveness contained in the SEC requirements. Public companies have invested significant amounts of time in documenting and testing their internal control over financial reporting. Controls are identified relating to each relevant management's assertion that is contained in the financial statements. Financial statement assertions, which are briefly defined next, relate to each account contained in the financial statements:

- *Existence or occurrence.* This assertion addresses whether assets or liabilities of the organization exist at a given date and whether recorded transactions have occurred during a given period.

- *Completeness.* This assertion addresses whether all transactions and accounts that should be presented in the financial statements are so included.

- *Rights and obligations.* This assertion addresses whether assets are the rights of the organization and liabilities are obligations of the organization at a given date.

- *Valuation or allocation.* This assertion addresses whether asset, liability, net asset, revenue, and expense components have been included in the financial statements at appropriate amounts.

- *Presentation and disclosure.* This assertion addresses whether particular components of the financial statements are properly classified, described, and disclosed.

For example, take the pledges receivable account typically found as an asset of a not-for-profit organization. Assume this account is significant to the financial statements. In presenting this account in the financial statements, management is making these assertions about this account: The pledges actually exist, all valid pledges have been recorded, the organization has the legal right to these pledges, pledges are properly valued and properly classified in the financial statements, and any required disclosures have been made. Now overlay the five components of internal control of the COSO internal control framework discussed earlier in this chapter. If each of the five components had just one relevant control related to each of the five assertions, there would be 25 controls to identify, document, and test for this one account. In practice, some of the internal control components may overlap with other financial statement accounts, reducing the number of controls to identify, or may simply not be relevant. On the other hand, the control activities component of the COSO internal control framework may have many controls related to just one assertion for the one account, greatly increasing the number of controls to identify, document, and test. Also consider that the not-for-profit organization may operate in a number of different locations where controls may need to be separately evaluated. Finally, consider that this process is repeated each year—although the first year is by far the hardest in terms of identifying and documenting the internal controls.

Suffice to say, this is a time-consuming, complicated process to be undertaken by the not-for-profit organization. Many public companies have sought outside assistance in performing this assessment of their internal control over financial reporting. Not-for-profit organizations desiring to implement these requirements should be prepared to make a significant investment in resources (definitely in staff and management time and probably in monetary resources for some outside assistance) to have a successful implementation. This is certainly not meant to discourage not-for-profit organizations from implementing these requirements. Rather, the purpose is to encourage not-for-profits to obtain an understanding of the extent of the undertaking before committing to implementation.

In addition to management's report on internal control, Section 404 requires the independent auditor of the financial statements to report on management's assessment of internal control. The Public Company Accounting Oversight Board's

AS-2 provides the requirements for independent auditors when they evaluate and report on management's assertions about internal control and how to report on those assertions. Exhibit 3.2 provides a sample report that would be issued by an independent auditor using the guidance of AS-2, assuming no material weaknesses in internal control were found and that the COSO internal control framework was used to evaluate controls. This example also assumes that the independent auditor followed all of the requirements of AS-2 and agreed to report under those requirements, so as to give the audit committee member an understanding of the level of assurance obtained under Section 404.

Note that some of the terminology used to describe what the independent auditor is performing can sometimes be confusing. Under professional standards, the independent auditor is actually performing what is known as an *attestation engagement*, in which he or she is attesting to the assertions that management is making in its report on internal control—that is, that the internal control over financial reporting is effective. AS-2 describes this process as an audit of internal control, the result of which is the attestation as to management's assertions. In

---

Exhibit 3.2   Report Expressing an Unqualified Opinion on Management's Assessment of the Effectiveness of Internal Control over Financial Reporting and an Unqualified Opinion on the Effectiveness of Internal Control over Financial Reporting

---

Report of Independent Public Accounting Firm

We have audited management's assessment, included in the accompanying *Report of Management on the Effectiveness of Internal Control over Financial Reporting* that XYZ Not-for-Profit Organization maintained effective internal control over financial reporting as of June 30, 20X1, based on criteria established in *Internal Control— Integrated Framework* issued by the Committee of Sponsoring Organizations of the Treadway Commission (COSO). XYZ Not-for-Profit Organization's management is responsible for maintaining effective internal control over financial reporting and for its assessment of the effectiveness of internal control over financial reporting. Our responsibility is to express an opinion on management's assessment and an opinion on the effectiveness of the organization's internal control over financial reporting based on our audit.

We conducted our audit in accordance with standards of the Public Company Accounting Oversight Board (United States). Those standards require that we plan and perform our audit to obtain reasonable assurance about whether effective internal control over financial reporting was maintained in all material respects. Our audit included obtaining an understanding of internal control over financial reporting, evaluating management's assessment, testing and evaluating the design and operating effectiveness of internal control, and performing such other procedures as we considered necessary in the circumstances. We believe that our audit provides a reasonable basis for our opinion.

An organization's internal control over financial reporting is a process designed to provide reasonable assurance regarding the reliability of financial reporting and the

Exhibit 3.2   Report Expressing an Unqualified Opinion on Management's Assessment of the Effectiveness of Internal Control over Financial Reporting and an Unqualified Opinion on the Effectiveness of Internal Control over Financial Reporting (continued)

preparation of financial statements for external purposes in accordance with generally accepted accounting principles. An organization's internal control over financial reporting includes those policies and procedures that (1) pertain to the maintenance of records that, in reasonable detail, accurately and fairly reflect the transactions and dispositions of the assets of the organization; (2) provide reasonable assurance that transactions are recorded as necessary to permit preparation of financial statements in accordance with generally accepted accounting principles, and that receipts and expenditures of the organization are being made only in accordance with authorizations of management and directors of the organization; and (3) provide reasonable assurance regarding prevention or timely detection of unauthorized acquisition, use, or disposition of the organization's assets that could have a material effect on the financial statements.

Because of its inherent limitations, internal control over financial reporting may not prevent or detect misstatements. Also, projections of any evaluation of effectiveness to future periods are subject to the risk that controls may become inadequate because of changes in conditions, or that the degree of compliance with the policies or procedures may deteriorate.

In our opinion, management's assessment that XYZ Not-for-Profit Organization maintained effective internal control over financial reporting as of June 30, 20X1, is fairly stated, in all material respects, based on criteria established in *Internal Control—Integrated Framework* issued by the Committee of Sponsoring Organizations of the Treadway Commission (COSO). Also, in our opinion, XYZ Not-for-Profit Organization maintained, in all material respects, effective internal control over financial reporting as of June 30, 20X1, based upon criteria established in *Internal Control—Integrated Framework* issued by the Committee of Sponsoring Organizations of the Treadway Commission (COSO).

We have also audited, in accordance with the standards of the Public Company Accounting Oversight Board (United States), the financial statements of XYZ Not-for-Profit Organization, and our report dated July 31, 20X1, expressed an unqualified opinion.

other words, both of these terms, "attestation" and "audit of internal control," describe the same service being provided by the independent auditor.

Audit Committee Considerations

In reviewing the basics of the not-for-profit organization voluntarily complying with the requirements of Section 404, an audit committee member might be immediately inclined to have the organization comply with these requirements. After all, this fairly lengthy chapter of this book has been devoted to internal control over financial reporting, meaning that it is an important area for audit committees. Don't the audit committee and the governing board members benefit by having management perform this assessment of internal control over financial reporting, and having an auditor give an opinion on this assessment? Wouldn't this assist the audit committee and the governing board (and management, for that matter) in meeting their responsibilities relating to financial reporting? Many would agree that the answers to these questions would be yes. However, the additional question that must be answered is: Will the additional costs to the not-for-profit organization outweigh whatever benefit is deemed to be derived by voluntary compliance with the requirements? Again, costs include both monetary as well as the investment of time of the staff and management of the not-for-profit organization. Monetary costs would include the fees of the independent auditor to perform the audit of internal control, plus other potential fees in assisting management with performing its assessment of the internal controls over financial reporting.

So far, these questions have assumed an all-or-nothing approach to Section 404 compliance. But because the not-for-profit organization's compliance is voluntary, it has the option to pick and choose those aspects of Section 404 that it implements. For example, the audit committee and governing board may decide that it is important for management to prepare its report on internal control, but that it is not necessary to have the assertions in this report audited by the independent auditor. If there are concerns about internal control in one particular aspect of the organization (such as the recording of contributions receivable, or perhaps payroll) the controls might be assessed relating to these areas, with additional areas phased in over future years. In addition, the independent auditor does not have to comply with the requirements of AS-2 in performing these procedures. The not-for-profit organization can discuss with the independent auditor alternatives to using this standard that might be more cost-effective.

Audit committees should also consider the size and complexity of the particular not-for-profit organization to determine whether voluntary compliance with Section 404 (or some variation of compliance) makes sense. It would seem harder to justify voluntary compliance in very small organizations with very simple accounting transactions compared with much larger organizations with high-volumes and more complex types of transactions. In addition, audit committees may also want to consider the past experience with the organization with internal control problems. If a not-for-profit organization has had many internal problems in the past, voluntary compliance with Section 404 might help it identify those areas where controls are lacking so that it can improve its overall internal control over financial reporting.

Public perception is another factor to consider. Would donors expect that the organization voluntarily comply with Section 404? Are other not-for-profit organizations of similar size in similar fields voluntarily complying with Section 404? In addition, audit committee and board members who are associated with publicly traded companies subject to the Section 404 requirements might feel exposed to a greater level of risk with a not-for-profit organization that doesn't take any steps toward increased monitoring of internal control over financial reporting.

The important point to take away from this section is not a definitive answer to whether it is appropriate for the organization to voluntarily comply with Section 404 or some variation thereof. Given the broad diversity of the size, type, complexity, and so on of not-for-profit organizations, this would be impossible to do.

Rather, this discussion is meant to provide audit committee members with a general understanding of the Section 404 requirements so that they can intelligently discuss whether compliance with these requirements makes sense for their particular organization.

BEST PRACTICE

Audit committees of not-for-profit organizations should consider whether some or all of the requirements of Section 404 of the Sarbanes-Oxley Act should be complied with by the organization and its independent auditor. The benefits of complying with some or all of the requirements should be weighed against the costs of compliance to the organization.

SUMMARY

This chapter has presented audit committee members with a number of best practices relating to internal control over financial reporting. The various components of internal control were discussed, along with their impact on financial reporting. In addition, the very important topic of management override of internal control over financial reporting was addressed. Finally, the various considerations that an audit committee might make in evaluating whether it would be appropriate for a not-for-profit organization to comply with some or all of the requirements of Section 404 of the Sarbanes-Oxley Act relating to internal control were addressed.

Chapter 4

Understanding and Addressing the Risks of Fraud

Many of the well publicized accounting scandals that have occurred in recent years involve fraudulent activities on the part of management or others within the organization. These events have brought into focus the audit committee's role in preventing and detecting fraud. Best practices for audit committees require that their roles in these areas be active and ongoing.

This chapter will provide audit committee members with an understanding of the topic of fraud, along with the factors that might increase the risks that fraud is occurring. The following topics will be covered:

- Definition of fraud
- Audit committee's role in preventing and detecting fraud
- Fraud risk factors to consider

The guidelines given in this chapter will assist audit committees in developing and applying best practices regarding fraud for their own particular not-for-profit organizations.

DEFINITION OF FRAUD

Fraud can be defined as a willful misrepresentation of the facts. But that may be too simplistic to be useful, so consider the definition of fraud in *Black's Law Dictionary*, which is included in the American Institute of Certified Public Accountants (AICPA) Audit Committee Toolkit (the AICPA Toolkit):

> An intentional perversion of truth for the purpose of inducing another in reliance upon it to part with some valuable thing belonging to him, or to surrender a legal right. A false representation of a matter of fact, whether by words or by conduct, by false or misleading allegations, or by concealment of that which should have been disclosed, which deceives and is intended to deceive another so that he shall act upon it to his legal injury.

> A generic term, embracing all multifarious means which human ingenuity can devise, and which are resorted to by one individual to get advantage over another by false suggestions or by suppression of truth, and includes all surprise, trick, cunning, dissembling, and any unfair way by which another is cheated.

This definition of fraud is very broad. It encompasses areas that would have only indirect effect on an organization's financial statements. For example, assume a not-for-profit organization sells tickets to its fund-raising dinner at $250 each. It indicates to donors that the actual value of the meal they will receive is $25, meaning that ticket purchasers can deduct $225 for each ticket they buy as a charitable contribution on their tax return. In fact, however, the not-for-profit organization knows that the actual value of the dinner is $75, but wants to give the dinner attendees the largest tax deduction possible. Is this fraudulent activity? Probably, yes. Is this fraudulent activity that the audit committee should be concerned about? Probably, yes—but only to the extent that noncompliance with the Internal Revenue Service would result in some financial harm to the not-for-profit organization.

What types of fraud should audit committees be concerned about? Fraud that results in a material misstatement of the not-for-profit organization's financial statements. (Note that audit committees are also concerned about errors that result in material misstatements of the financial statements.) The distinguishing feature of fraud, however, is that it is an intentional act that results in a material misstatement of the financial statements.

Audit committees are concerned about fraud in basically the same way that independent auditors of the financial statements are concerned about fraud—specifically, regarding fraud that results in a material misstatement of the financial statements. Independent auditors use a relatively new auditing standard in addressing the risk of fraud in an audit of financial statements. This standard is the Statement on Auditing Standards No. 99, "Consideration of Fraud in a Financial Statement Audit" (SAS-99), which defines the types of fraud that auditors are concerned with and discusses various risk factors that auditors should be aware of in order to identify situations at an organization being audited where certain factors are present that might increase the risk of fraud occurring. These risk factors, which also send up important warning flags to audit committee members, will be discussed in the last section of this chapter.

SAS-99 defines two types of financial statement misstatements that are relevant to the consideration of fraud:

1. Misstatements arising from fraudulent financial reporting
2. Misstatements arising from misappropriation of assets

The following brief overview of these types of misstatements due to fraud should assist audit committee members in understanding the types of areas that warrant their diligence.

Misstatements Arising from Fraudulent Financial Reporting

These are intentional misstatements or omissions of amounts or disclosures in the financial statements that are designed to deceive financial statement users, and where the effect causes the financial statements not to be presented, in all material respects, in conformity with generally accepted accounting principles (GAAP).

SAS-99 points out the following ways in which fraudulent financial reporting can be accomplished:

- Manipulation, falsification, or alteration of accounting records or supporting documents from which financial statements are prepared
- Misrepresentation in or intentional omission from the financial statements of events, transactions, or other significant information
- Intentional misapplication of accounting principles relating to amounts classifications, manner of presentation, or disclosures

Another aspect of fraudulent financial reporting is a little more of a gray area than these fairly straightforward methods. It involves an aggressive application of an accounting principle that produces the desired accounting result without having to resort to recording phony journal entries in the accounting ledgers. The point at which this aggressiveness crosses the line to become fraudulent is a matter that needs to be addressed in the individual circumstances at hand.

Misstatements Arising from Misappropriation of Assets

This type of fraud is sometimes called theft, or *defalcation*. It involves the theft of an organization's assets, the effect of which is to cause the financial statements not to be presented, in all material respects, in conformity with GAAP. Misappropriation of assets can occur in a number of different ways, including embezzling receipts, stealing assets, or causing an organization to pay for goods or services that were not received by the organization.

FRAUD IN RELATION TO FINANCIAL REPORTING

One thing that should be clear from reading the definition of the two types of fraud as given in the auditing standards used by independent auditors is that the independent auditor is concerned about fraud that would cause the financial statements not to be presented, in all material respects, in conformity with GAAP. In other words, auditors don't assume the responsibility of uncovering all frauds that may be occurring in a not-for-profit organization. Under SAS-99, their responsibility is to "plan and perform the audit to obtain reasonable assurance about whether the financial statements are free of material misstatement, whether caused by error or fraud." For a number of years, independent auditors have been battling what they perceive as an "expectation gap" between what they believe their responsibility regarding fraud is and what the public at large believes it to be. Although auditing standards, such as SAS-99 and an earlier fraud auditing standard, provided additional guidance to auditors on how to plan and perform their audits relative to fraud, the basic premise has essentially remained unchanged—that is, that auditors are responsible only for planning and performing their audits to obtain reasonable assurance that the financial statements are not materially misstated due to fraud or unintentional errors. Responsibilities for auditors who do uncover fraud (regardless of whether it is material to the financial statements) have also been clarified, and these will be discussed in a later chapter.

THE AUDIT COMMITTEE'S ROLE IN PREVENTING AND DETECTING FRAUD

The audit committee's role in preventing and detecting fraud can be viewed as the committee itself being part of the not-for-profit organization's internal control over financial reporting. As such, it will have an interest in fraud that results in material misstatements of the organization's financial statements that portend to be presented in conformity with generally accepted accounting principles, similar to the independent auditor of the financial statements. But the audit committee's responsibilities as to fraudulent financial reporting or misappropriation of assets can go beyond those of an independent auditor. First, as stated in the heading for this section, the audit committee has a role in *preventing and detecting* fraud. In contrast, the independent auditor has no real role in fraud *prevention*; their role is one of fraud *detection*. Second, the audit committee should be concerned about instances of fraud beyond those that have a material impact on the not-for-profit organization's financial statements.

As part of the control environment of a not-for-profit organization, the audit committee should be aware of the various situations and circumstances that have allowed any fraud to be perpetrated. For example, could an immaterial instance of fraud point to weaknesses in an organization's internal control such that larger, material frauds could be committed? Let's say that a national not-for-profit membership organization with 100 local chapters discovers that one of the chapters has incurred a liability to a conference center—the local chapter has no funds to pay for the center. The local chapter leadership has deliberately failed to report this liability to the national organization, although it is clear that the national organization will have to pay the liability incurred by the local chapter. This one instance may not even closely approach having a material effect on the financial statements of the national not-for-profit organization, but what if all 100 chapters had similar liabilities that were not reported? The answer may be very different as to whether material liabilities have been incurred and not reported in the national organization's financial statements. In this situation, upon learning of the one instance of an unauthorized liability being incurred, and financial information being deliberately withheld to hide this liability, the audit committee should make inquiries of the management of the national organization as to what steps they have taken to make sure that this situation does not reoccur in the future.

BEST PRACTICE

Audit committee members should understand that they are a part of the not-for-profit organization's internal controls to prevent or detect fraud and, therefore, should conduct their activities with this objective in mind.

The AICPA Toolkit describes the role of the audit committee in ensuring that the organization has antifraud programs and controls in place to help prevent fraud; and in the event of its discovery, to properly fulfill their duties, which include:

- Monitoring the financial reporting process.
- Overseeing the internal control system.
- Overseeing the internal audit and independent accounting functions.
- Reporting findings to the board of directors.

In other words, the audit committee's role relating to fraud isn't an isolated action, whereby the audit committee takes a few preventive steps and is done with it. No, the audit committee's role is a pervasive one that affects all of its responsibilities relating to the financial statements, internal controls, and the internal and external audit programs that are in place at the organization. That means preventing and detecting fraud must involve all of the audit committee's activities.

As would an auditor, an audit committee member should approach this area with a sense of professional skepticism. Fraud, by its nature, involves a deception or a misstatement of the truth. Professional skepticism doesn't mean that the audit committee member must always assume that the management or others within the organization are lying to them. Paraphrasing the SAS-99 requirements for auditors, audit committee members should approach their work with a questioning mind and a critical assessment of evidence presented. A risk of fraud occurring could be present regardless of any past experiences with the not-for-profit organization or the audit committee members' beliefs about the honesty and integrity of management.

BEST PRACTICE

Audit committee members should maintain a healthy degree of professional skepticism in performing their activities and interacting with management and others within the not-for-profit organization.

FRAUD RISK FACTORS TO CONSIDER

The risk of fraud, including fraud that results in a material misstatement of the financial statements, is present in virtually all organizations, including not-for-profit organizations. SAS-99 contains a useful list of fraud risk factors that auditors should consider when evaluating the fraud risk level of an organization, for the purpose of performing an audit of financial statements. Audit committee members can benefit from familiarizing themselves with these risk factors, not because their responsibilities are the same as independent auditors of financial statements, but because they need to be aware of circumstances within and outside the not-for-profit organization that might indicate a greater likelihood that fraud is occurring there. Again, the audit committee's concern is in regard to fraud that would cause a material misstatement of the financial statements, as well as fraud that might indicate there are significant internal control deficiencies within the not-for-profit organization.

SAS-99 points to three conditions that are generally present when fraud occurs:

- *Incentive.* Management or other employees have an incentive, or are under pressure, which provides them with a reason to commit fraud.
- *Opportunity.* Circumstances exist (such as the absence of controls or the ineffectiveness of controls) that provide an opportunity for a fraud to be perpetrated.
- *Rationalization.* Those involved in the fraud are able to rationalize committing the fraudulent act.

It's also important to note that these factors can lead otherwise honest people to commit fraud. Although the attitude and ethical values of certain individuals enable them to intentionally commit fraud without qualms, sometimes otherwise honest people may commit fraud when an environment exists that imposes sufficient pressure on them. The greater the incentive or pressure, the more likely an individual will be able to rationalize the acceptability of committing fraud.

At the same time audit committee members should be aware of the following risk factors, they also should keep in mind that almost implicit in the act of committing fraud is the concealment of the fraud from others, including management (assuming they are not the ones committing the fraud) and the governing board and audit committee. Fraud may be concealed by withholding evidence, misrepresenting information in response to inquiries, or falsifying documentation. Fraud may also be concealed through collusion among management, employees, and/or outside parties. Through collusion, false evidence that controls have been operating effectively may be presented to management and/or internal and external auditors. In addition, consistent misleading information may be given to explain an unexpected result in the reporting of financial information.

Given that concealment of fraud is contingent on the party or parties committing the fraud, audit committee members should maintain open lines of communication with individuals within the not-for-profit organization who don't have a direct responsibility for the preparation of financial statements, such as the fundraising executive or the internal audit director. When the existence of any of the fraud risk factors described next is present, the audit committee should consider broadening these communication lines.

The risk factors given here are based on those provided by SAS-99 to external auditors, but modified for not-for-profit organizations. Note that while certain of the SAS-99 fraud risk factors don't directly relate to not-for-profit organizations (such as the effect of fraudulent actions on the value of stock options), often present in not-for-profit organizations are operations that are fee-based and generate revenue, such as tuition for students. The risk factors relating to financial performance would therefore apply to both not-for-profit organizations and commercial enterprises. These examples are categorized by incentives, opportunities, and rationalizations relating to misstatements arising from fraudulent financial reporting:

- *Incentives/pressures.* Financial stability or profitability is threatened by economic, industry, or organization operating conditions, such as:
  - High degree of competition, or market saturation, accompanied by declining margins
  - High degree of competition for contributions by organizations in similar programmatic fields
  - High vulnerability to rapid changes, such as technology, product or program obsolescence, or interest rates
  - Significant decline in customer or program service client demand, and increasing numbers of failures of other not-for-profit organizations in similar fields or failures in the overall economy at large
  - Operating losses, making the threat of bankruptcy, foreclosure, or undesired merger with another organization imminent
  - Recurring negative cash flows from operations, or an inability to generate cash flows from operations while reporting increases in fee revenues or contributions
  - Rapid growth or unusual profitability, especially compared to that of other organizations in the same programmatic fields
  - New accounting, statutory, or regulatory requirements

Excessive pressure exists for management to meet the requirements or expectations of third parties due to the following:

- Profitability or trend-level expectations of current and potential donors, significant creditors, or other external parties, including expectations created by management in overly optimistic press releases, annual report messages, or fund-raising appeals.
- Need to obtain additional debt or other financing to stay competitive, including financing of major research and development or capital expenditures
- Marginal ability to meet debt repayment or other debt covenant requirements
- Perceived or real adverse effects of reporting poor financial results on significant pending transactions, such as contract awards or a significant donor contribution

Available information indicates that management's (or others') personal financial situation is threatened by the organization's financial performance, arising from the following:

- Significant financial interests in the organization
- Significant portions of their compensation being contingent upon achieving aggressive targets for operating results, fund-raising levels, financial position, or cash flow
- Personal guarantees of debts of the organization

Excessive pressure on management or operating personnel to meet financial targets set up by the governing board or management, including revenue, fund-raising, or profitability goals.

- *Opportunities.* The nature of the industry or the organization's operations provides opportunities to engage in fraudulent financial reporting, which can arise from the following:
  - Significant related-party transactions not in the ordinary course of business or with related organizations not audited or audited by a different firm of independent auditors
  - A strong financial presence or ability to dominate a certain industry sector, enabling the organization to dictate terms or conditions to suppliers or customers that may result in inappropriate or nonarm's-length transactions
  - Assets, liabilities, revenues or expenses that are based on significant estimates that involve subjective judgments or uncertainties that are difficult to collaborate
  - Significant, unusual, or highly complex transactions, especially those close to period-end, that pose difficult "substance over form" questions
  - Significant operations located or conducted across international borders in jurisdictions whose business environments and cultures are different
  - Significant bank accounts or subsidiary or branch operations in locations for which there appears no clear business justification

  Ineffective monitoring of management is a result of the following:
  - Domination of management by a single person or small group without compensating controls
  - Ineffective governing board oversight over the financial reporting process and internal control

  There is a complex or unstable organizational structure, as evidenced by the following:
  - Difficulty in determining the structure or individuals that control the organization
  - Overly complex organizational structure involving unusual legal entities or managerial lines of authority
  - High turnover rate of senior management, counsel, or board members

  Internal control components are deficient as a result of the following:
  - Inadequate monitoring of controls, including automated controls and controls over interim budget-to-actual reporting
  - High turnover rates or employment of ineffective accounting, internal audit, or information technology staff
  - Ineffective accounting and information systems, including situations involving reportable conditions

- *Rationalizations/attitudes.* Risk factors reflective of attitudes/rationalizations by governing board members, management, or employees that allow them to engage in and/or justify fraudulent financial reporting may not be easy to observe or identify. However, audit committee members may become aware of the following behavior that may indicate a fraud risk factor is present:

- Ineffective communication, implementation, support, or enforcement of the organization's values or ethical standards by management; or the communication of inappropriate values or ethical standards
- Nonfinancial management's excessive participation in or preoccupation with the selection of accounting principles, or the determination of significant estimates
- Known history of violations of laws or regulations, or claims against the organization, its senior management, or governing board, alleging fraud or violations of laws and regulations
- Excessive interest by management in maintaining or improving the organization's performance indicators, such as the ratio of program expenses to total expenses
- A practice by management of committing to donors, creditors, and other parties to achieve aggressive or unrealistic forecasts
- Management failure to correct known reportable conditions on a timely basis
- An interest by management in employing inappropriate means to minimize reported unrelated business income taxes
- Recurring attempts by management to justify marginal or inappropriate accounting on the basis of materiality
- The relationship between management and the current or predecessor independent auditor is strained, as exhibited by the following:
  - Frequent disputes with the current or predecessor auditor on accounting, auditing, or reporting matters
  - Unreasonable demands on the auditor, such as unreasonable time frames in which to complete the audit or to issue the auditor's report
  - Formal or informal restrictions on the auditor that inappropriately limit access to people or information or the ability to communicate effectively with the governing board or the audit committee
  - Domineering management behavior in dealing with the auditor, especially involving attempts to influence the scope of the auditor's work or the selection or continuance of personnel assigned to or consulted on the audit engagement

In addition to the preceding risk factors regarding fraudulent financial reporting, there are also risk factors contained in SAS-99 related to misstatements of financial statements arising from the misappropriation of assets. These risk factors are also categorized by incentives/pressures, opportunities, and attitudes/rationalizations, and have been modified to apply to not-for-profit organizations. They are as follows:

- *Incentives/pressures*
  - Personal financial obligations may create pressure on management or employees with access to cash or other assets susceptible to theft to misappropriate those assets.

- Adverse relationships between the organization and employees with access to cash or other assets susceptible to theft may motivate those employees to misappropriate those assets. For example, adverse relationships may be created by:
  - Known or anticipated future employee layoffs
  - Recent or anticipated changes to employee compensation or benefit plans
  - Promotions, compensation, or other rewards inconsistent with expectations

- *Opportunities.* Certain characteristics or circumstances may increase the susceptibility of assets to misappropriation. For example, opportunities to misappropriate assets increase when the following are present:
  - Large amounts of cash on hand or processed
  - Inventory items that are small in size, of high value, or in high demand
  - Easily convertible assets, such as bearer bonds, diamonds, or computer chips
  - Fixed assets that are small in size, marketable, or lacking observable identification of ownership

  Inadequate internal control over assets may increase the susceptibility of misappropriation of those assets. For example, misappropriation of assets may occur because of the following:
  - Inadequate segregation of duties
  - Inadequate management oversight of employees responsible for assets; for example, inadequate supervision or monitoring of remote locations
  - Inadequate job applicant screening of employees with access to assets
  - Inadequate record keeping with respect to assets
  - Inadequate system of authorization and approval of transactions, such as the purchasing function
  - Inadequate physical safeguards over cash, investments, inventory, collections, or fixed assets
  - Lack of complete and timely reconciliations of assets
  - Lack of timely and appropriate documentation of transactions
  - Lack of mandatory vacations for employees performing key control functions
  - Inadequate management understanding of information technology, which enables IT employees to perpetrate a misappropriation
  - Inadequate access controls over automated records, including controls over and review of computer systems event logs

- *Rationalizations/attitudes.* Risk factors reflective of employee attitudes and rationalizations that allow them to justify misappropriation of assets are difficult for audit committee members to observe. However, audit committee members may become aware of the following attitudes or behavior of employees who have access to assets susceptible to misappropriation:

- Disregard for the need for monitoring or reducing risks related to misappropriations of assets

- Disregard for internal control over misappropriation of assets by overriding existing controls or by failing to correct known internal control deficiencies

- Behavior indicating displeasure or dissatisfaction with the organization or its treatment of the employee

- Changes in behavior or lifestyle that may indicate assets have been misappropriated

Audit committee members reading some of these risk factors may be asking themselves how they could ever become aware when these risk factors exist, given that they don't have day-to-day interaction with the not-for-profit organization's employees who perform important, but low-level, control functions. This is indeed a good question, but audit committee members can obtain information about fraud risk factors from a number of sources, other than direct observation; and this listing can serve as a basis for questioning whether management believes some of these conditions exist. In addition, interaction with the not-for-profit organization's internal audit function, if one exists, as well as the independent auditors, can also provide insight into the various risks of fraud that might be present at a particular not-for-profit organization. The independent auditors should be communicating any areas that they consider to be particularly troubling, including revenue recognition, which auditors are required to treat as an area of fraud risk, irrespective of the organization's particular circumstances. Moreover, audit committee members can go beyond simply listening to what the independent auditor highlights as fraud risks and ask: (1) Were some or all of the fraud risk factors listed here considered; and (2) why the auditor does or does not believe the fraud risk factor to be present. Such discussions can also serve to improve the two-way communications between the independent auditor and the audit committee members.

SUMMARY

This chapter presented background information on the types of fraud that should concern audit committee members. The audit committee's role in fraud prevention and detection was also discussed, along with the fraud risk factors with which audit committee members should be familiar to help increase their vigilance as to the risk of misstatement of the organization's financial statements due to fraud.

Chapter 5

Defining the Role of the Internal Audit Function

This chapter will describe the best practices for a not-for-profit's audit committee relating to the organization's internal audit function. First it must be noted that it is not always a given that an internal audit function exists within a not-for-profit organization. Many not-for-profit organizations are relatively small in size, hence may find it very difficult or not cost-effective to maintain an internal audit function. In contrast, internal audit functions are common in large not-for-profit organizations. For example, a Web search for internal auditing resources provides numerous links to quite impressive sites of internal audit departments at private colleges and universities. For purposes here, however, this chapter assumes that the not-for-profit organization for which audit committee best practices are being established is of sufficient size to warrant at least some form of internal audit function.

This chapter will cover the following specific information:

- Definition of an internal audit function
- Relationship of the audit committee to the internal audit function
- Internal audit function's role in supporting management's assertions about internal control

After reviewing these topics, audit committee members will have a broad enough understanding of the nature and role of the internal audit function to assist them in helping the not-for-profit organization maintain this role for the organization's particular circumstances.

DEFINITION OF AN INTERNAL AUDIT FUNCTION

The Institute of Internal Auditors (IIA) defines internal auditing as follows:

> Internal auditing is an independent, objective assurance and consulting activity designed to add value and improve an organization's operations. It helps an organization accomplish its objectives by bringing a systematic, disciplined approach to evaluate and improve the effectiveness of risk management, control, and governance processes.

The IIA's *International Standards for the Professional Practice of Internal Auditing* specify that an organization's chief audit executive (CAE) establish risk-based plans to determine the priorities of the internal audit activity, consistent with the organization's goals. The IIA further specifies that the audit risk assessment be reevaluated each year and that auditors' assessment results be disclosed to and discussed with the audit committee.

An internal audit function should be viewed as part of the internal control over financial reporting, which was discussed in Chapter 4. That said, internal control over financial reporting is not the only objective of an internal audit function. Traditional objectives of internal auditing include:

- Reliability and integrity of information
- Compliance with the organization's policies and procedures
- Safeguarding of assets
- Efficient and effective use of resources
- Evaluation of the organization's operational goals, to determine if they have been accomplished

In other words, internal auditors are interested in more than simply whether a particular organization has good internal control over its financial accounting and reporting. Internal auditors are also interested in whether the particular organization is using its resources efficiently, and to that end may conduct audits designed to develop recommendations as to how certain operations or processes can be improved to the benefit of the organization. These operations or processes may or may not have a direct impact on the organization's accounting and financial reporting operations.

The discussion of the IIA definition and standards apply to a formal internal audit function within an organization in which the CAE develops a risk-based audit plan to guide the internal audit function's activities during an annual period. In designing an audit plan for the next year's internal audit activities, the changes to the risks faced by the particular organization since the prior year are considered, along with the results of the prior year's audit, so that the audit plan for the upcoming year focuses on those risks the organization still must address. In other words, careful thought and consideration is given as to how to effectively and efficiently apply the resources of the internal audit function (i.e., the auditors) to most favorably benefit the organization. This means that the internal auditors do not simply keep performing the same audits or types of audits year after year with little or no regard as to the relevancy of these audits.

The reason that it is important to keep these practices in mind when considering a particular not-for-profit organization's internal audit function is that there can be many different types of activities that are called "internal audit" but that are far removed from the activities of an effective internal audit function as just described. The point is that audit committee members cannot "lay back" upon being informed that a not-for-profit organization has an internal audit function. No, they should take the time and make the effort to understand exactly how that function operates (as discussed in the next section), so that they can rely justifiably on the activities of the internal audit function.

Audit committee members may come in contact with not-for-profit organizations that have one or two internal auditors. It is entirely possible that such a small internal audit function may operate as described by the IIA standards above, including the performance of annual risk assessments and development of effective audit plans. It is also possible, however, that these internal auditors may not be performing internal audit work in the traditional sense described. Often, in small to midsized organizations, internal auditors are really part of an internal control process, rather than an independent evaluator of that process. For example, the internal auditor's function may consist entirely of making sure that the appropriate documentation is in place before a disbursement is made. The internal auditor's sign-off on a disbursement before it is made is part of the internal control process, rather than an objective review to ascertain whether the complete control process over disbursements has been operating effectively as designed.

Not-for-profit organizations are notorious for keeping their administrative staffing levels at a bare-bones level. This makes them susceptible to falling into practice of using any available internal audit staff to supplement the accounting staff, rather than using the internal auditors to perform true audit functions. The accounting functions assigned to internal auditors may look like audit functions, which is a way to justify their use. The preceding example of the internal auditor reviewing disbursement documentation can certainly be called "auditing disbursements." In some cases, the types of disbursements subject to the internal auditor's review may be more limited, such as applying only to those disbursements that represent a reimbursement of travel and entertainment expenses incurred by senior management of the organization. In other cases, internal auditors may be given the responsibility to audit expenditures made under a capital program that is being undertaken by the not-for-profit organization. Perhaps internal auditors are used to verify change orders to contracts presented by construction contractors performing services under a capital program.

Don't misunderstand: Having any of these functions performed by individuals labeled as internal auditors is not necessarily a bad thing. The point is simply to encourage audit committee members to determine whether the not-for-profit organization has an internal audit function in the classical sense of the term. The nature of the not-for-profit organization will influence that function's interaction with the audit committee, which is the topic of the next section.

RELATIONSHIP OF THE AUDIT COMMITTEE TO THE INTERNAL AUDIT FUNCTION

The reporting of an internal audit function has long been an important topic in ensuring that the function operates effectively within the organization. The heart of the matter is whether the CAE reports at a high enough level within the organization to ensure that the results of audit activities of the internal audit function receive the proper attention within the organization. Although the internal audit function exists to benefit the organization, as just discussed, the nature of audit activities is to recommend improvements to current processes or practices, which often involves criticism of the current procedures and practices. If the CAE reported to a member of management, that person could cause negative audit findings to be suppressed in order to protect management from criticism by the governing board or the audit committee. In discussing the reporting relationship of the CAE, what's really being considered is the reporting relationship of the entire internal audit function, since it is assumed that the entire internal audit function reports to the CAE.

A fundamental concept of internal auditing is that it is objective in nature. A reporting structure that would allow management to compromise that objectivity would call into question the objectivity of the audit function, thereby diminishing its value to those who depend upon it. A proper reporting relationship of the CAE becomes even more important where there are situations of fraud involving management. The CAE needs a direct mechanism to report such activities to the governing board through the audit committee. For practical purposes, however, the CAE would have to report to some high level of management within the organization for day-to-day administrative purposes.

BEST PRACTICE

The CAE should have a direct reporting relationship to the audit committee of the not-for-profit organization. The CAE may report to a senior member of management for administrative matters.

The reporting relationship between the CAE and the audit committee should be more than just a line on an organization chart. It is important that the CAE and the audit committee communicate frequently and on a regular basis. The CAE should meet with the audit committee members at each scheduled meeting of the committee. The CAE also should be empowered to contact the audit committee (most practically by contacting the audit committee chair) at any time, if necessary, to make the chair of the audit committee aware of any audit findings that the CAE deems worthy of immediate attention. Finally, the CAE should review the annual audit plan with the audit committee and its members on the results of the audits that have been performed.

As evidence of the importance of open lines of communication between the CAE and the audit committee, the AICPA's Audit Committee Toolkit recommends that the CAE meet with the audit committee members in executive session at each of the committee's meetings. These executive sessions, which would occur without members of management present, would allow the CAE to openly inform the audit committee members of any concerns that he or she has, without having to express these concerns before management. At the same time, the audit committee members would be able to express their concerns to the CAE, without the discomfort of management being present. This information can be very useful to the CAE in developing future audit plans, while giving the audit committee members an opportunity to use the internal audit function as a means to obtain direct, hands-on information about the various functions and processes within the not-for-profit organization.

BEST PRACTICE
_____

The CAE should meet frequently with the audit committee members; an executive session attended by members of the audit committee and the CAE should be held in conjunction with these meetings.

As previously stated, however, if the reporting relationship is more form than substance (that is, it's just a line on the organization chart), having the internal audit function report directly to the audit committee won't be effective. In order for the audit committee to really be in control of the internal audit function, it must take an active role in managing that function. To make sure that the audit committee's role is an active one, consider doing the following to solidify the audit committee's role relative to the internal audit function.

- *Consult the audit committee before a CAE is appointed or dismissed.* Whereas the day-to-day personnel functions of the not-for-profit organization must be administered by the management of the organization, the audit committee should be given an opportunity to meet with CAE candidates before anyone is approved. This not only establishes the audit committee as an important factor in the individual's employment, but it also ensures the audit committee as to the qualifications and skill sets of the individual who is appointed to this position. In addition, before a CAE is dismissed or reassigned by management, the audit committee should be informed by management of the reasons for the dismissal or reassignment. The audit committee also should hold an exit interview with any departing CAE to clearly identify the reasons for his or her leaving— specifically, to ensure they do not involve any type of cover-up of management problems.
- *Have the audit committee review the adequacy of the resources of the internal audit function.* Again, the not-for-profit organization's management has the primary responsibility to allocate its budgeted dollars among its various programmatic and administrative areas. Because an effective internal audit function is seldom listed in any not-for-profit organization's mission statement, the internal audit function will usually find itself competing for resources with the organization's other administrative areas. Even worse, because the internal audit function does not actually "produce" a line function (such as paying bills, reconciling bank accounts, collecting receivables, etc.) internal audit resources are often the first to go when budget times turn rough. In the best of cases, the internal audit function's role in fostering the not-for-profit organization's operational efficiency will spare it from budget cuts. Barring that, the

audit committee should insist that an adequately staffed internal audit function is maintained in accordance with the size and complexity of the individual not-for-profit organization.

- *Assure that the audit committee is satisfied with the professional and technical capabilities of the individuals comprising the internal audit function.* It's important that the audit committee be confident that the internal audit staff have the appropriate technical qualifications and levels of experience, are adequately trained and supervised, and are periodically evaluated on their performance. The audit committee should also be cognizant that different skill sets may be required for internal audit function staff. For example, for a not-for-profit organization that is heavily dependent on information technology for processing program, financial, or other data, the audit committee should inquire whether an appropriately trained IT auditor has been employed and whether sufficient IT audits are being performed.

- *Have the audit committee review the internal audit department functioning.* The internal audit function itself has its own set of procedures and processes that ensure its effective operation. For example: A process should be in place to perform the annual risk assessment and develop the annual audit plan; individual audits need to be scheduled and have resources allocated to them; the status of all ongoing audits must be reviewed periodically; audit reports have to be drafted and finalized; audit results must be communicated to all interested parties; and so on. The audit committee does not have to be involved in all of these details, but it should inquire about the processes and procedures being used and be satisfied that the internal audit function operates effectively. Furthermore, the audit committee should be briefed as to the status of all of these activities during its periodic meetings with the CAE. When the results of a specific audit are going to be reviewed at a particular audit committee meeting, it may be useful to have the audit team members who performed the audit present so that the audit committee members can improve their understanding of the audit procedures, problems encountered, recommendations developed, and so on.

- *Have the audit committee review the results of any peer reviews performed of the internal audit function.* Some internal audit functions voluntarily undergo a peer review of their audit operations every few years, similar to the peer reviews required of independent auditors. The audit committee can play a role in deciding whether such a peer review would be considered necessary and cost-effective for the internal audit function of the particular not-for-profit organization. If a peer review is performed, the audit committee should be made aware of the results of the review and informed of any corrective action that needs to be taken by the internal audit function to resolve any reported deficiencies in its operations or procedures.

Before leaving the topic of the audit committee's relationship with the not-for-profit organization's internal audit function, two additional topics need to be addressed:

- Importance of management resolution of audit findings
- Outsourcing the internal audit function

Each of these topics is addressed in turn.

Importance of Management Resolution of Audit Findings

At first glance, this topic may be too obvious to warrant discussion, but the audit committee should assess the importance management places on resolving issues that result from audits performed by the internal audit function. An internal audit function may be performing terrific audits, but if management is not doing anything to correct problems identified and to implement recommendations, the resources of the internal audit department are being wasted. Yes, performing the audits may provide management and the audit committee with some comfort that material deficiencies in the areas audited do not exist; however, it's essential that the recommendations made by the auditors be implemented by management on a timely basis—assuming management agrees with them. If management doesn't agree with the recommendations, these disagreements should be reviewed by the audit committee to see if they can negotiate some mutually agreeable solution to the problem, leaving all parties confident that the particular problem is being addressed. It does little good for management and the audit committee when internal auditors periodically audit a particular area and find the same deficiencies recurring over and over. The correct solutions should be agreed upon and implemented within a reasonable period of time.

Management's attention to correcting deficiencies noted by the internal audit function also gives the audit committee members a sense of how aware management is of internal control issues. This was discussed at length in Chapters 3 and 4, regarding, respectively, an organization's control environment and management's ability to override internal control. Obviously, when management takes internal audit findings seriously and addresses them on a timely basis, the audit committee members can be confident that management is interested in maintaining effective internal control within the organization.

Outsourcing the Internal Audit Function

Perhaps the preceding discussion of audit committee activities has caused you to think that this is a fairly complex area, and why not just hire someone to do it for you. Be aware that others have thought of this, too. In fact, internal audit outsourcing services were being promoted by independent auditing firms even prior to the Sarbanes-Oxley Act, which focused so much attention on accounting regulation and internal control. A precise definition of outsourcing as it relates to the internal audit function is hard to arrive at, because a not-for-profit organization and an outside auditor can enter into many different types of agreements that involve some form of internal audit outsourcing.

The audit committee has a clear interest in its not-for-profit organization's decision to outsource its internal audit function. Obviously, the cost of these outside services needs to be evaluated, and then compared with the costs of maintaining the internal audit function within the organization. A discussion of this decision is, however, beyond the scope of this book, in particular because it must be evaluated on a case-by-case basis. What is within the scope of this book is the audit committee's involvement in the decision-making process to determine whether some or all of the organization's internal audit function should be outsourced. And if the decision is made to outsource, the audit committee should then evaluate whether the firm hired can remain independent of the not-for-profit organization so that it could also audit the organization's financial statements.

BEST PRACTICE

The audit committee should concur with any decision to outsource some or all of the internal audit functions of a not-for-profit organization.

If an outsourcing option is chosen by the not-for-profit organization, regardless of the scope of the contract, the overall responsibility for maintaining effective internal control, which includes the internal audit function, still resides with the not-for-profit organization, its governing board, and its audit committee. Accordingly, the audit committee should continue to review and analyze issues similar to those discussed previously, regardless whether these activities are performed by members of the staff of the not-for-profit organization or by a third-party vendor.

INTERNAL AUDIT FUNCTION'S ROLE IN SUPPORTING MANAGEMENT ASSERTIONS ABOUT INTERNAL CONTROL

Whether a not-for-profit organization implements any or all of the requirements of the Sarbanes-Oxley Act, a discussion of the internal audit function of an organization would not be complete without mention of the role that the internal audit function can play in assisting with management's assertions about the internal control over financial reporting of an organization.

As discussed in Chapter 4, Section 404 of the Sarbanes-Oxley Act requires management to develop and monitor procedures and controls for making the required assertion about the adequacy of internal control over financial reporting, along with the required attestation by the independent auditor of management's assertions. The IIA, in a paper titled "Internal Auditing's Role in Sections 302 and 404 of the U.S. Sarbanes-Oxley Act of 2002" (hereafter, the "IIA Section 404 paper") addresses the role that internal auditors can plan in assisting management in fulfilling these responsibilities. (Section 302 of Sarbanes-Oxley requires quarterly certification by management not only of financial reporting controls, but also disclosure controls and procedures—a topic beyond the scope of this book.) The IIA concludes that it is management's responsibility to ensure that an organization is in compliance with these requirements; this responsibility cannot be delegated or abdicated. However, the IIA concludes that support for management in the discharge of these responsibilities is a legitimate role for internal auditors. If a not-for-profit organization decides to voluntarily comply with the requirements of Section 404, it has greater flexibility in the use of the internal audit function in meeting these requirements.

However, management and the internal audit function may choose to comply with the IIA's recommendation that the internal audit function role in a particular organization's Sarbanes-Oxley implementation can be significant, but also must be compatible with the overall mission and charter of the internal audit function. Regardless of the level and type of involvement selected, it should not impair the objectivity and capabilities of the internal audit function for covering other risk areas within the organization. In other words, the internal audit function should not be required to eliminate or drastically scale back work that would have been performed under a risk-based audit approach in order to assist management in complying with the Sarbanes-Oxley requirements.

The IIA recommends that the CAE make sure that the audit committee is kept up to date on the role and activities of the internal audit function with regard to implementing the requirements of Section 404. Any instances where the internal audit function's activities might impair the function's independence or objectivity should be discussed with the audit committee prior to the performance of activities. The audit committee should also be apprised of the current and potential future impacts of devoting the internal audit function's resources to assisting in Section 404 compliance efforts.

The audit committee may be very comfortable with devoting internal audit resources to providing assistance to management in performing its assessment of internal control over financial reporting. One could argue that whatever work the internal audit function performs in this area provides a benefit to the internal control over financial reporting of the organization, even if the efforts of the internal audit function are reduced in other areas. On the other hand, since the implementation efforts of a not-for-profit organization attempting to comply with the requirements of Section 404 can be substantial, there is a danger that the resources of the internal audit function will be completely used up in assisting management develop its assertions regarding the organization's internal controls over financial reporting. This can result in important risk areas, identified by the CAE and discussed with the audit committee, going unaudited by the internal audit function. The point is not to decide how much of the internal audit resources to use in complying with Section 404, but that the use of internal audit resources to assist management in this compliance be discussed with and approved by the audit committee. Furthermore, the audit committee should monitor on an ongoing basis how the internal audit function resources are being used. This will enable audit committee members to gain an understanding of other risk areas that are not being audited by the internal audit function, as well as ensuring that the work being done by the internal auditors to assist management on Section 404 compliance are appropriate and not affecting the internal audit function's overall objectivity and independence.

BEST PRACTICE

The audit committee should review and approve plans to use internal audit resources to assist management in forming its assertions about internal control when a not-for-profit organization is voluntarily implementing the requirements of Section 404 of the Sarbanes-Oxley Act.

To assist internal auditors, management, and audit committees in determining an appropriate role for the internal audit function in Section 404 compliance, the IIA Section 404 paper lists the following activities as part of the internal auditor's recommended role. These activities are categorized into the following phases of the project: project oversight, consulting and project support, ongoing monitoring and testing, and project audit. The IIA reiterates that management is responsible for implementing the processes necessary to meet the regulatory requirements of Sarbanes-Oxley. The role of the internal auditor should support management in carrying out its assertions. The term "responsibility" needs to be viewed in a slightly different context when a not-for-profit organization is voluntarily implementing the requirements of Section 404, because management does not have a legal responsibility to provide its assertions about the organization's internal control over financial reporting. Rather, management is accepting these responsibilities voluntarily. Once management provides the assertions about internal control over financial reporting, there should be no doubt that these are the assertions of management, not others, such as the internal audit function. The activities of the internal audit function suggested by the IIA Section 404 paper are as follows:

- Project oversight
  - Participate on the project steering committee to provide advice and recommendations to the project team, and monitor progress and direction of the project.
  - Act as the facilitator between the independent auditor and management.
- Consulting and project support
  - Provide existing internal audit documentation for processes under the scope of the Section 404 project.
  - Advise on best practices, such as documentation standards, tools, and test strategies.
  - Support management and process owner training on project and risks and control awareness.
  - Perform quality assurance review of process documentation and key controls prior to handoff to the independent auditor.
- Ongoing monitoring and testing
  - Advise management regarding the design, scope, and frequency of tests to be performed.

- Use an independent assessor to evaluate management testing and assessment processes.
- Perform tests of management's basis for assertions.
- Perform effectiveness testing for high reliance by independent auditors.
- Aid in identifying control gaps, and review management plans for correcting control gaps.
- Perform follow-up reviews to ascertain whether control gaps have been adequately addressed.
- Act as coordinator between management and the independent auditor as to discussions of scope and testing plans.
- Participate on the disclosure committee to ensure that results of ongoing internal audit activities and other examination activities, such as external regulatory examinations, are brought to the disclosure committee for consideration.

- Project audit
  - Assist in ensuring that organization initiatives are well managed and have a positive impact on the organization. The assurance role supports senior management, the audit committee, the governing board, and other stakeholders.
  - Use a risk-based approach in planning the many possible activities regarding project audits. Audit best practices suggest internal auditors should be involved throughout a project's life cycle, not just in postimplementation audits.

Full use of the internal audit function in all of these areas in likely to be beyond the capabilities of the internal audit function in all but the larger not-for-profit organizations. However, the purpose of reviewing this list is not to lay out a specific plan for an internal audit function, but to provide a general understanding of the types of activities it would be appropriate for the internal audit function to perform.

It is also important that the audit committee members be assured that the internal audit function's objectivity and independence are not impaired. To that end, the IIA Section 404 paper provides the following general factors when considering appropriate roles for the internal audit function:

- *Responsibility for specific operations results in a presumption of impairment of objectivity regarding that operation.* Whether an internal auditor has taken on responsibility for a specific operation will depend on the situation. In general, internal auditors who actively participate in making or directing key management decisions will have impaired objectivity.

- *An internal auditor's objectivity is not impaired when the internal auditor recommends standards of control for systems or reviews procedures before they are implemented.* The auditor's objectivity is considered to be impaired if the internal auditor designs, installs, drafts procedures for, or operates such systems.

- *Consulting on internal control matters is a normal role for internal auditors and does not impair independence or objectivity.* However, making key management decisions does impair the internal auditor's independence or objectivity.

- *Devoting specific amounts of effort to a nonassurance activity may not impair independence.* That said, the CAE should consider the impact (including risk) of performing nonassurance activities for completing the otherwise planned assurance engagements.

In addition to these general factors, the IIA Section 404 paper describes the following specific types of services that the internal audit function may be requested to provide, along with the implications of providing those services.

Internal Audit Function as a Source of Consultants

Internal auditors acting in a consulting capacity may be asked to assist the organization in identifying, evaluating, and implementing risk and control assessment methodologies, as well as recommending controls to address the related risks. Decisions as to whether to adopt or implement these recommendations should be made by management.

An internal auditor may be asked to participate in the design and implementation of a new process for management to assess the not-for-profit organization's internal control over financial reporting. If the auditor's activities are limited to evaluating the new processes and defining a reference guide on recommended controls, the internal auditor's objectivity is not likely to be impaired. And if the internal auditor serves on a project team that selects the assessment methodology and tools, and selects or defines the documentation standards management will use, objectivity is also not likely considered impaired. However, if the internal auditor implements new processes to remediate control gaps, the internal auditor's objectivity may be considered impaired.

Internal Audit Function as a Source of Resources for Documentation and Testing

The internal audit function may be requested to aid management in documenting internal controls. If, however, the internal auditor works closely with management in documenting controls and "slides" into more of a decision-making role (such as implementing internal controls during the documentation process), then objectivity will be impaired.

The internal audit function may aid management in the design or execution of control effectiveness. It is recommended that the degree to which the internal audit function constitutes management's testing of controls be clearly specified and agreed to by management, the internal audit function, and the audit committee. In all cases, management should make the final decision on control design and operating effectiveness, whether and what to remediate, and whether information produced, from which their assertions are to be made, is sufficient.

Internal Audit Function as the Source of the Lead Project Manager

An internal auditor may be asked to take on the role of lead project manager for all or part of the efforts related to compliance with the requirements of Section 404. A project manager is generally responsible for monitoring the progress of the project, arranging for appropriate communication of project results during the course of the project, and monitoring adherence to the timetable that has been established. If the internal auditor's role is restricted to these administrative tasks, objectivity would not likely be impaired. But if the project manager's role extends to include: serving as the primary decision maker as to acceptability of work product, approving successful completion of stages of the project, authorizing redirection of resources within the project team, or performing similar types of management activities, the internal auditor's objectivity would be impaired.

Internal Audit Function as a Source of Training or Information about Controls

Internal auditors may provide training and/or information on internal control identification and assessment, risk assessment, and test plan development without an impairment to objectivity.

Internal Audit Function as a Source of Control Self-Assessment

Internal control self-assessment may be used as an effective and efficient means for management to document and or assess internal control. If an internal auditor provides information or training or facilitates an internal control self-assessment, objectivity is not likely to be impaired. If the internal auditor takes ownership of the internal control self-assessment, however, or is the main source of documentation, then objectivity would be impaired.

Internal Audit Function as a Certifier in the Disclosure Process

The internal audit function may be asked to complete some types of certifications or to issue an opinion on internal control as part of management's Section 404 compliance. The CAE should ensure that any certification or opinion is supported by adequate, appropriate audit evidence to support the certification or opinion, as required by standards of audit and conduct normally used by internal auditors.

Again, the internal audit function professionals are in the best position to determine whether any activity they are asked to perform as part of management's implementation of Section 404 would impair their objectivity or independence. The CAE should ensure that the audit committee is kept informed about the role and activities of the internal audit function relating to Section 404 compliance. Any instances where objectivity might be impaired by the role of the internal audit function should be discussed by the CAE with the audit committee prior to the internal audit function assuming the role. The implications and impact to both current and future internal audit plans from using internal audit function resources on Section 404 compliance should also be discussed. In instances where it is determined the internal audit function's objectivity is impaired, the CAE, the governing board, and the audit committee should consider how this impairment affects the ability of the internal audit function to perform future internal audit engagements.

SUMMARY

The internal audit function of a not-for-profit organization can be a very important resource to the organization's audit committee in fulfilling its responsibilities. The audit committee should be an active manager in determining how internal audit function resources are used. It should take an active role in reviewing audit plans, analyzing audit results, and ensuring that the internal audit function has adequate resources and access to organizational operations to effectively perform its functions. Executive sessions with the not-for-profit organization's CAE can provide valuable insights to the audit committee regarding the not-for-profit organization's operations and its internal control. In addition, the internal audit function can be a valuable resource to the management of a not-for-profit organization that is voluntarily implementing the provisions of Section 404 of the Sarbanes-Oxley Act. In such organizations, the audit committee must play an important role in verifying that work performed by the internal audit function does not impair its objectivity or independence and that the work doesn't deplete the resources of the internal audit function to such an extent that audits to be conducted under the internal audit plan are neglected or are not performed, to the detriment of the not-for-profit organization.

Chapter 6

Establishing an Effective Whistleblower Program

This chapter will explore best practices that audit committees of not-for-profits can use to put effective whistleblower programs in place at their organizations. At organizations where significant accounting and financial reporting fraud has been revealed, it has been employees of those organizations who have proven instrumental in bringing those activities to light. As reported in Chapter 3 on internal control, management override of internal control is an important issue for audit committees. An effective whistleblower program is one mechanism that can increase the probability that inappropriate management override of internal control will be detected.

Despite the benefits of an effective whistleblower program, it is unlikely that this topic would have warranted its own chapter (albeit a short one) in a book on audit committee best practices were it not for the passage of the Sarbanes-Oxley Act. That act has very specific requirements relating to whistleblower programs for audit committees of public companies, and this chapter will review those requirements and suggest areas where not-for-profit organizations can adopt best practices to help them institute effective whistleblower programs. In addition, this chapter will examine one of the provisions of the Sarbanes-Oxley Act that relates directly to whistleblowers and that must be complied with, even by not-for-profit organizations. Audit committees of these organizations will certainly be interested in this provision.

SARBANES-OXLEY REQUIREMENTS FOR AUDIT COMMITTEES RELATIVE TO WHISTLEBLOWERS

The basic objective of the requirements of the Sarbanes-Oxley Act for audit committees relative to whistleblowers is to provide a process audit committee can implement to assure that complaints about accounting, internal control, and auditing matters directly, are being handled appropriately—and without these matters being filtered by management. Further, the Sarbanes-Oxley Act provides safeguards for whistleblowers, to prevent retaliation against them by the organization.

The requirements of Sarbanes-Oxley relative to whistleblowers are contained in Section 301, which relates to audit committees. The requirements state:

Each audit committee shall establish procedures for—

(a) the receipt, retention, and treatment of complaints received by the issuer regarding accounting, internal accounting controls, or auditing matters; and

(b) the confidential, anonymous submission by employees of the issuer of concerns regarding questionable accounting or auditing matters.

At first read, these requirements may sound simple to implement. However, consider a typical large Fortune 500 organization with operations in many locations, both domestic and international. Also consider that the audit committee is comprised of individual members who are independent of the organization. These individuals attend meetings on a part-time basis and usually don't have a physical presence within the organization. How would such an audit committee receive anonymous complaints from employees, and how would they address and track each of these complaints? What resources would they use to investigate whether the complaints they are receiving are valid?

The answer is that the audit committee must establish an infrastructure that would allow complaints to be compiled, analyzed, responded to, documented, and stored. Some organizations have begun using the services of outside vendors that can provide the infrastructure for these processes. Why? Because the premise of the Section 301 rule is that audit committees must establish the process directly, they must be cognizant that they can't establish a process that allows management to influence which complaints to "filter out" of the process, either by management or other employees in the organization. That's what makes it difficult to handle complaints using the resources of the organization itself and why hiring a third-party contractor to perform the administration of the whistleblower program can be attractive.

Audit committees of not-for-profit organizations are not required to abide by the exact requirements of Section 301. However, in establishing best practices for audit committees, it makes a lot of sense to install a mechanism by which the audit committee can directly receive and investigate complaints received from whistleblowers. So, without strict compliance with Section 301, the not-for-profit organization audit committee may find that it is excessive or too expensive to hire an outside service to administer the program. Instead, audit committee members may be more comfortable with a program that uses resources of the not-for-profit organization to address these complaints, provided controls are in place to make sure that all complaints are made available for the audit committee's review—that is, without certain comments being filtered out.

Another factor to keep in mind in setting up a whistleblower program is that probably a broad range of complaints are likely to be received, particularly when those lodging the complaints feel that their anonymity would be protected. The challenge for the audit committee is to sift through the complaints and identify those that have merit. These "legitimate" complaints are likely to be interspersed with many others that could be considered frivolous. In addition, because of personal vendettas, misinformation, speculation, and misunderstanding, many complaints may, simply, be false. The audit committee cannot assume that every complaint it receives is valid and warrants its full attention. On the other hand, the audit committee must be vigilant in considering all complaints, hence must have the aforementioned established process for sorting through all of the complaints for the purpose of identifying those that warrant further investigation.

The Institute of Internal Auditors (IIA) has published a paper as part of its Implementation Guide Series. Titled "Section 301.4—Complaints (Whistleblowing)," hereafter, the IIA Whistleblower Paper, it provides many useful suggestions for building an effective whistleblower program. The IIA Whistleblower Paper discusses the factors that contribute to employee disclosures and then introduces the steps that an organization can take to establish an effective whistleblower program. Although a program established using these guidelines would probably be beyond what would be required for a typical not-for-profit organization, which tend to be much smaller than publicly traded companies, many of the ideas can be adapted for use by the audit committees of not-for-profit organizations.

The IIA Whistleblower Paper identifies the following factors that encourage employees to disclose information in a whistleblower program:

- *Protection.* Employees are likely to be concerned that they will be subject to various forms of retaliation, including discrimination, harassment, intimidation, alienation, target supervision, or termination if they blow the whistle on one or more fellow employees or superiors. Management must ensure their employees that such actions will not be taken against them. In addition, there are legal safeguards, discussed in the second part of this chapter, that protect employees from retaliation, and employees should be made aware of these protections.

- *Accessibility.* The easier it is for employees to disclose a complaint, the better the chances that they will take the opportunity to make the disclosure.

- *Tone at the top.* This topic was covered in an earlier chapter, as part of the control environment discussion, as a component of internal control. Management must send clear and consistent messages that employees should behave ethically, act with integrity and fairness, and comply with the law. When management affirms it will not tolerate questionable behavior, and follows this principle itself, it is more likely that employees will expect the same behavior of fellow employees and report instances where this is not the case.

- *Strong support network.* This factor acknowledges that whistleblowers often struggle emotionally with whether or not they should disclose the wrongdoing they witnessed. A supportive work environment, the fostering of teamwork, supportive professional and community service initiatives, and effective publicizing of the whistleblower program can raise the comfort level of whistleblowers, enabling them to make the disclosure or complaint.

- *Awareness.* Employees have to know the program exists and that it has the support of management; and they must know what to do if they encounter a questionable situation.

There are four steps in establishing a whistleblower program, as described in the IIA Whistleblower Paper. They are as follows:

1. *Assessment.* This step involves evaluating the characteristics of the organization and its employees to determine the needs that a whistleblower program would have to address. For example, consider the following factors:
   a. *Geographical dispersion.* Identify the locations where the organization has a presence, then make sure all employees have access to the program.
   b. *Linguistic groups.* If many employees in the organization do not speak English, address this fact in the design of the whistleblower program.
   c. *Program access.* Make access to the whistleblower program free (or at least very inexpensive) and simple to use. For example, enable employees to file complaints using toll-free telephone numbers, faxes, or email. The ability to fax enables the employee to send any documentation they think is appropriate and necessary. Consider setting up an email address that does not identify the individual who will read the email, but instead has a generic name that indicates it is for the receipt of whistleblower complaints.
   d. *Staffing.* As described previously, the staffing for the whistleblower program can be provided by the not-for-profit organization itself, or a third-party vendor may be hired to administer the program. Regardless, make the program available at all times, every day of the year. Smaller organizations can rotate individuals who are "on call," such as by the use of cell phones, to handle calls as they come in. Naturally, those handling the complaints should be trained to do so in a professional manner, making sure that needed relevant facts are obtained from the whistleblower.
   e. *Performance protocol.* Assign case numbers for each complaint and provide guidance for when complaints need to be escalated to higher levels or handled in a tighter time frame, depending on the nature of the complaint.
   f. *Oversight board.* Establish an oversight board to ensure that complaints are being handled appropriately, as well as to add credibility to the program.
   g. *Manager responsibilities.* Give the manager of the program a reasonable amount of resources to administer the program, with sufficient independence and access to senior management. Periodic meetings between the manager and the oversight board should take place to discuss disclosures made under the whistleblower program and the results of those disclosures.
2. *Building.* This phase of the whistleblower program involves the actual setup of the physical hardware and putting individuals in place to perform and administer the program. This phase is divided into two areas:
   a. *Training.* Properly train all individuals involved in the program (including telephone operators who take calls from whistleblowers).
   b. *Policies and procedures.* Make the whistleblower program part of the organization's policies and procedures, and treat it as part of the organization's internal control.
3. *Releasing.* The third phase of establishing a whistleblower program is to release the whistleblower program throughout the organization. There are many different ways that the program can be released, such as by a memorandum to

employees, emails, videoconferencing, computer-based training, and others. However, the IIA Whistleblower Paper states that the most effective way to release the program is through meetings with employees. In this way, employees will gain a better appreciation of the importance of the program and a sense of management's commitment to it; moreover, they can have their questions answered immediately. The meetings should include identifying the methods available for disclosing concerns and the existence of an oversight board, to ensure privacy and the effectiveness of the operation of the program. It is also recommended that the program be released at the same time throughout the organization.

4. *Performance monitoring.* The fourth phase of establishing a whistleblower program is performance monitoring, which should be designed to verify compliance with the program's established protocol to ensure quality control. It consists of:

   a. *Monitoring.* Monitoring is performed through the periodic meetings held by the oversight board and the program manager. Critical developments should be brought to the audit committee's attention immediately. All complaints or concerns relating to accounting, internal accounting controls, or auditing matters should be reported periodically to the audit committee.

   b. *Employee surveys.* Annual anonymous surveys can provide much information about employees' awareness of the program's purpose, effectiveness, and weaknesses. Surveys also remind employees about the existence of the program.

These four phases suggested by the IIA Whistleblower Paper provide a very useful overview of the types of considerations a not-for-profit organization's audit committee should evaluate when working with the organization to establish a whistleblower program. Again, because exact compliance with Section 301 provisions is not required, not-for-profit organizations have a lot of flexibility as to how a whistleblower program can be established. Given that many not-for-profit organizations are small to medium in size, the whistleblower program described here would likely need to be phased down to the appropriate scale. But don't misunderstand: Downsizing a program is not the same as instituting an ineffective program; rather, it is designing a good program given the size of the organization and its available resources.

An audit committee's primary concerns involve accounting and financial reporting, internal control over financial reporting, and auditing matters. And though an organization's whistleblower program should be broad enough to capture employee disclosures in areas other than those, the audit committee may choose to establish its own procedures to address its special needs, particularly in smaller and midsized organizations. The following are some ideas that may be useful in designing the "right-size" whistleblower program at a not-for-profit organization, to specifically address an audit committee's needs:

- Set up an email address, telephone extension with voicemail capabilities, or post office box specifically designated to accept complaints related to accounting and financial reporting, internal control over financial reporting, auditing matters, and fraud.

- Instruct the not-for-profit organization to include information about the program in the introductory materials provided to new hires of the organization.
- Encourage the not-for-profit organization to publicize the existence of the program through employee meetings; and to post the email address, telephone extension, or post office box number set up to receive complaints on bulletin boards, in newsletters, and so on, so that they are widely available and known to employees.
- Ensure that the email, voicemail, or post office box can be checked periodically by a designated member of the audit committee, who can then advise the full audit committee of complaints received. This assignment may be made on a rotating basis among audit committee members, so that it never becomes burdensome for any one person. This assignment might also be given to a senior management member, but having an audit committee member do it, if possible, minimizes the risk that management will filter the complaints before they get to the audit committee. After all, if an employee believes that it is important for him or her to communicate a complaint directly to the audit committee, it may be because that complaint is either about activities of management or because management has not seen the need to address the particular complaint.
- Enable the audit committee member reviewing the complaints to perform a quick sort of the complaints received into several categories, such as:
  - Frivolous, requiring no further action other than to pass the complaint on to management, if appropriate
  - Potentially important, requiring investigation and follow-up
  - Serious, requiring immediate attention because of some impending transaction that could cause financial harm to the organization if not handled expeditiously.

For complaints falling into the latter two categories, the audit committee can discuss them with management or, if the resource is available, with the organization's internal audit function for investigation and follow-up. Again, the urgency with which the complaint must be dealt with will vary. If someone is alleged to be stealing money from the organization, this complaint should be addressed quickly. If someone is alleged to have deliberately misstated an accounting entry for depreciation expense, the complaint should be addressed before the next set of financial statements are issued for the organization.

How the not-for-profit organization's management, governing board, and audit committee decide to structure the whistleblower program will determine how it is implemented at that particular organization. The audit committee members should be comfortable that the whistleblower program is set up in an effective manner and meets the stated goals. The specifics of how the program is established must be determined on an individual basis for each not-for-profit organization. There is no one-size-fits-all program applicable to all not-for-profit organizations. What's important is that a program be established and that it employ as many of the concepts described in this chapter, along with additional concepts as necessary, to meet the needs of the particular organization.

BEST PRACTICE

The audit committee should work with management of the not-for-profit organization to design and implement an effective whistleblower program.

PROTECTING WHISTLEBLOWERS FROM RETALIATION

One of the most important characteristics of a whistleblower program is that any employee who makes a complaint must feel assured that they will not be retaliated against for doing so. If a complaint is made anonymously by an employee, the employee must be confident that his or her anonymity will be preserved. Likewise, if the employee chooses to identify him- or herself in making the complaint, he or she must be able to trust that management or others within the organization will not take any retaliatory actions to his or her detriment.

It must be made clear in communicating the program to the employees of the organization that retaliation against whistleblowers will not be tolerated by the management, governing board, or audit committee. Unfortunately, employees may be disinclined to trust such assurances, and there may have to be one or more instances that prove this to be the case before other employees come to trust that they will indeed be protected from retaliation.

Audit committee members should also keep in mind that retaliation can take many forms. Firing or demoting an employee immediately after they lodge a complaint to the whistleblower program may be an obvious sign that retaliation has taken place. But other forms of retaliation may be more subtle. For example, whistleblowers may be passed over for promotions or salary increases, or may be given less favorable assignments than they would have received had they not filed a complaint to the whistleblower program. Numerous other forms of subtle retaliation may be directed at the whistleblowing employee, and the point is that all types of retaliation should be considered when designing a program, to prevent it.

The not-for-profit organization not only needs to prevent retaliation to make the whistleblower program effective, it also needs to protect itself from legal action by an employee who believes that he or she is being retaliated against. On the other hand, the not-for-profit organization can't be in the position that it has to provide so much legal protection to an employee that it compromises its right to terminate an employee for reasons totally unrelated to the whistleblowing incidence. Establishing rules for how retaliation against whistleblowers is handled should be done with legal counsel, to ensure that the appropriate rights of both the employees and the not-for-profit organization are preserved. (Such considerations are outside the scope of this book.)

BEST PRACTICE

The not-for-profit organization, with appropriate legal counsel, should establish policies and procedures that protect employees participating in the whistleblower program from retaliation.

There is one section of the Sarbanes-Oxley Act that applies to *all* types of organizations, including not-for-profits. It deals with retaliation against an employee who provides a law enforcement officer with information relating to the commission of a federal offense. Section 1107, "Retaliation Against Informants," amends Section 1513 of title 18 of the United States Code by appending the following language to that section:

> (e) Whoever knowingly, with the intent to retaliate, takes any action harmful to any person, including interference with the lawful employment or livelihood of any person, for providing to a law enforcement officer any truthful information relating to the commission or possible commission of an Federal offense, shall be fined under this title or imprisoned not more than 10 years, or both.

Note that this provision of the Sarbanes-Oxley Act relates specifically to information provided to a law enforcement officer regarding the commission of a federal offense; therefore it obviously doesn't provide broad protection for employees under a not-for-profit organization's whistleblower program. Nevertheless, the design and implementation of an organization's whistleblower program should ensure that compliance with Section 1107 is incorporated into the whistleblower program. This provision of the Sarbanes-Oxley Act also should be considered when developing the policies and procedures to protect the rights of whistleblowers, as just discussed.

SUMMARY

A not-for-profit organization and its audit committee should develop an effective program to encourage employees to report inappropriate activities through a whistleblower program. The program should ensure that all legitimate complaints are given the proper attention by management and, if necessary, the audit committee and/or the governing board. Furthermore, employees participating in a whistleblower program should be given adequate protection from retaliation as a result of providing information through the whistleblower program.

Audit Committee's Relationship with the Independent Auditor

One of the most important parties outside the not-for-profit organization with which the audit committee has frequent contact is the independent auditor. The audit committee's role with respect to the organization's financial reporting and internal control over financial reporting is deeply intertwined with the independent auditor's role of issuing an opinion as to whether the not-for-profit organization's financial statements are presented in accordance with generally accepted accounting principles (GAAP). The independent auditor views the audit committee as part of the internal control over financial reporting of the not-for-profit organization, and the audit committee looks to the independent auditor to provide its opinion as to whether its financial statements are presented in accordance with GAAP, as well as to provide comments about the not-for-profit organization's internal control over financial reporting.

This chapter will describe several aspects of the audit committee's relationship with the independent auditor and provide background material intended to assist audit committee members in learning more about the independent audit process, so they can better communicate with the independent auditor. Specifically, the following topics will be addressed:

- Defining the broad relationship of the audit committee and the independent auditor.
- Procuring the services of an independent auditor.
- Understanding how independent auditors audit financial statements.
- Monitoring the independence of the independent auditor.
- Interpreting communications received from the independent auditor.
- Soliciting optional attestation as to management's assertions regarding internal control over financial reporting.

Audit committee members cannot employ best practices to maximize their use of the not-for-profit organization's independent auditor unless they first gain a general understanding of the audit process. Further, it is essential to establish the relationship between the independent auditor and the audit committee, to ensure that the audit committee opens an effective line of communication with the independent auditor.

DEFINING THE BROAD RELATIONSHIP OF THE AUDIT COMMITTEE AND THE INDEPENDENT AUDITOR

Traditionally, independent auditors were hired by management of not-for-profit organizations, with varying degrees of input into the process by the governing board and the audit committee. And, typically, as long as the independent auditor's service was satisfactory, the same audit firm was reappointed year after year. At the same time, not-for-profit organizations could select from a virtual smorgasbord of additional services offered by the independent auditor, from tax consulting and Form 990 preparation to actuarial calculations for pensions and postretirement benefits (other than pensions) to accounting and other systems installations. Perhaps the independent auditor also provided "client assistance" work, consisting of providing staff on a temporary basis to perform accounting or internal audit functions.

As the use of past tense in the first paragraph implies, some of the practices described there are no longer in common practice today. The changes can be attributed to shifts in the relationship between the audit committee and the independent auditor, and changes in the requirements for an auditor to be "independent" so as to issue an opinion on the financial statements of a not-for-profit organization.

The change in the relationship paradigm between an audit committee and an independent auditor was driven by the Sarbanes-Oxley Act, which has been referred to extensively throughout this book because of its impact on organizations, even those to which it does not directly apply, such as not-for-profit organizations. Basically, for public companies (issuers) in the following quotation, the Sarbanes-Oxley Act places the responsibility for managing the relationship with the internal auditor on the audit committee. Here is what Section 301 of Sarbanes-Oxley, which addresses the role of audit committees in public companies, says relative to the audit committee's responsibility for the independent auditor (referred to as the "registered public accounting firm"):

> The audit committee of each issuer, in its capacity as a committee of the board of directors, shall be directly responsible for the appointment, compensation, and oversight of the work of any registered public accounting firm employed by that issuer (including resolution of disagreements between management and the auditor regarding financial reporting) for the purpose of preparing or issuing an audit report or related work, and each such registered public accounting firm shall report directly to the audit committee.

It would be difficult to draft any language that more squarely places oversight of the independent auditor on the audit committee. In addition to its oversight role, the audit committee has the responsibility to appoint the independent auditor, as well as to come to terms with the audit firm regarding the audit fee.

Since the Sarbanes-Oxley Act does not directly apply to not-for-profit organizations, these organizations, including their governing boards and audit committees should evaluate and determine how the relationship between the audit committee and the independent auditor will be established for each particular organization. Frankly, the requirements covering the audit committee and the independent auditor contained in the Sarbanes-Oxley Act provide a good model that could serve as a best practice in many not-for-profit organizations. The following discusses what led to this conclusion, so that not-for-profit organizations and their audit committees can understand the reasoning behind it and provide guidance in those areas where modification of these requirements may be deemed necessary.

Appointment of an Independent Auditor

In the next section, best practices for not-for-profit organizations to consider in procuring the services of an independent auditor are addressed, but first we'll discuss whether this appointment should be a function of the audit committee. Historically, hiring an internal auditor was similar to many other types of contractual purchases made by a not-for-profit organization—that is, it was handled by the organization's management. Audit committees may or may not have approved of the selection.

As will be seen in the following section, procuring the services of an independent auditor can be a major undertaking, requiring the commitment of a significant amount of resources by whoever or whichever department is managing the procurement. And because a not-for-profit organization's audit committee does not generally have its own staff, it will likely have to rely on the staff of the not-for-profit organization to administer the selection of the independent auditor, even if the audit committee retains the final authority to make the appointment. An alternative to this approach is to have management make the selection of the independent auditor, then have the audit committee approve the selection. In these cases, the audit committee may require management to present to the audit committee the results of any scoring or evaluations prepared by those members of the not-for-profit organization participating in the selection. The audit committee may also ask to see a summary of the various proposals received from the various independent auditors seeking to perform the audit. The more removed from the evaluation process the audit committee is (i.e., the more it relies on management to evaluate prospective auditors), the less likely the audit committee members will feel as if they "own" the selection and that the independent auditor works on their behalf.

BEST PRACTICE

The audit committee should make the selection of the independent auditor and administer as much of the selection process as is practical.

Audit committee members should read and evaluate the proposals received from the prospective independent auditors, although the not-for-profit organization's staff should be expected to provide summary information about each of the proposals, to include the number of hours each prospective auditor expects to spend on the audit and its proposed audit fee. Audit committee members should also meet with and interview the "short list" of those audit firms, deemed the most qualified and at a reasonable price, before making a selection.

Retention of an Incumbent Auditor

Do not interpret the preceding discussion to mean that a new independent auditor is selected every year. Typically, independent auditors are hired under multiyear contracts. A common contract term is four years, although three- to five-year contracts are also appropriate. One reason for a multiyear contract is to encourage auditors to propose on the audit at lower fees. Independent auditors typically incur significant start-up costs in the first year of an audit but can generally provide better pricing to the not-for-profit organization under a multiyear contract, over which it can spread theses costs. Accordingly, an appointment decision does not have to be made every year. At the end of a multiyear contract, the audit committee members should evaluate whether they desire to keep the current independent auditor and negotiate a new contract, or—particularly if required by the not-for-profit organization's standard procurement practices—whether they need to request proposals from other auditors before deciding whether to retain the incumbent auditor or to make a change. This decision is one that should be made by the audit committee.

Retaining an incumbent auditor under a multiyear contract should occur without incident; nevertheless, the audit committee should determine whether the incumbent auditor is performing satisfactorily each year of the contract. If the independent auditor is not performing satisfactorily under the terms of its contract, the audit committee should express those concerns to the independent auditor to resolve these issues before proceeding to the next year. If the issues cannot be resolved, the audit committee may wish to explore whether the not-for-profit organization can terminate the contract with the independent auditor before its stated end. This step should be taken only as a last resort, and only after the services of the independent auditor have been deemed to be truly deficient.

PROCURING THE SERVICES OF AN INDEPENDENT AUDITOR

It can be very difficult for an audit committee member to effectively participate in the selection of an independent auditor if he or she is unfamiliar with how audit services are typically procured. Independent audit firms come in all sizes and configurations and have various levels of experience with not-for-profit organizations. Consideration of the many variables that factor into the selection process can greatly improve the chances of hiring an independent auditor that is the best match for the not-for-profit organization.

BEST PRACTICE

Audit committees of not-for-profit organizations should carefully evaluate potential auditors to ensure the selection of an independent auditor that best suits the needs both of the organization and the audit committee.

The following summarizes some of the common considerations involved in selecting an independent auditor. As in most cases, the size of the not-for-profit organization will greatly impact the extent of the selection process. The discussion here would generally apply to midsize to large not-for-profit organizations, those most likely to have audit committees. That said, these concepts can be used in selecting an independent auditor for smaller organizations as well, but with fewer steps.

Drafting a Request for Proposal

A request for proposal is a document sent by the not-for-profit organization to independent audit firms, asking for proposals to audit the financial statements of the organization. The management of the not-for-profit organization may issue the request for proposal, in which case it should indicate that it is doing so on behalf of its audit committee—assuming the audit committee is taking responsibility for hiring the independent auditor. The information typically included in a request for proposal is described in the following paragraphs. (Note: This information is not intended as a template for a request for proposal, although it could be used for that, but rather to give audit committee members an idea of some of the considerations that are normally made when evaluating audit firms as part of the procurement process.)

The request for proposal should serve a number of difference purposes. First, it should lay out the scope of work to be performed. For example, the following might be included in the scope of work section of the request for proposal:

- Number of years of audits that will be covered by the contract
- Deadlines for completing the audits
- Whether any special audit services will be required, such as a Single Audit, required when a not-for-profit organization receives a certain level of federal funding
- Whether the audit firm will be responsible for preparing the federal Form 990 and any state charities bureau registrations
- Any additional requirements that are known or anticipated that the auditor would have to perform

Second, the request for proposal can ask the independent auditor to provide certain information about the firm that would be necessary and useful for the audit committee and the not-for-profit organization to have in making its selection. For example, the following information might be requested:

- Size of the audit firm, including the number of professional staff and partners and the number of offices from which they operate
- A sample list of the audit firm's clients
- A sample list of not-for-profit organizations that are audit clients of the firm, including those similar in size and program function to the not-for-profit organization requesting the proposal (for example, charitable organizations, membership organizations, social clubs, political organizations, etc.)
- Names and backgrounds of the key individuals who will be assigned to the not-for-profit organization's audit (such as the partner, manager, and senior accountant)
- A copy of the audit firm's most recent peer review of its quality control system, including the related letter of comments and the audit firm's responses to those comments
- Names and telephone numbers of references at similar audit clients
- Perceived attributes of the audit firm that set it apart from other audit firms
- Proposed cost of performing the audits, including the number of hours, by staff level, anticipated for each year audited, along with the hourly rates being charged for each staff level; also, any anticipated out-of-pocket expenses in order to determine a total cost for each audit year from the proposal.

Third, the audit firm should be asked to provide a brief description of its audit approach to the not-for-profit organization. If the not-for-profit organization has multiple locations, the audit firm's approach to handling those locations should also be determined.

Finally, the request for proposal should discuss the process that will be used by the not-for-profit organization to evaluate the proposals it receives. The evaluation process described might include:

- Decision-making authority, which is the audit committee in this discussion
- Qualitative criteria that will used to evaluate the proposers, such as experience in the industry, quality of the audit team assigned to the audit, and results of the audit firm's peer review
- Quantitative criteria, providing some guidance as to the proposed audit fees among firms; for example, qualitative factors might be weighted 75 percent of the total evaluation points awarded, while cost is weighted 25 percent of the total evaluation points awarded
- A statement that personal interviews of the audit team are required and will be conducted by the audit committee
- An overview of the expected time frame in which the selection process will take place

You might be thinking that including all of these requirements in a request for proposal is being too specific as to what information is required of the audit firm. You might also be surprised at the depth of the information requested. Why not simply call three audit firms and ask them how much they would charge for the audits? Why not just let the firm tell us what they think is important and make the decision based on that information? For smaller not-for-profit organizations, these might be valid points and, as was stated at the beginning of this section, a more streamlined process might be appropriate. But for midsize to larger organizations, there are benefits to obtaining this level of information during the request for proposal process. First, it is not recommended that independent auditors be selected based solely on the fee they will charge for the audits. Particularly in the current environment, it is important that audit committee members be given some assurances that they are engaging a quality firm to audit the not-for-profit organization, and lowest price is not an indicator (at least not generally a positive indicator) of the quality of the work that an audit firm will perform. Second, when evaluating the proposals that are received, it will be important to have similar information for all of the firms being evaluated. This will enable the committee to compare "apples to apples" because the same types of information will be at hand for all of the firms under consideration.

Three additional considerations may be useful in defining the request for proposal. First, if a qualitative evaluation of the audit firm is to be an important element of the process, the request for proposal might specify that the audit cost proposals be submitted separately from the technical proposals. In this way, the technical scoring can be completed before the cost proposals are opened, which may lead to a more objective evaluation of the technical merits of each audit firm.

Second, you may want to limit the number of pages audit firms may submit in the technical request for proposal. Audit firms have been known to bury selection committees under reams of paper, much of which contains information that has simply been recycled from other proposals the audit firm has prepared, hence may be viewed as useless boilerplate language. Limiting the technical proposal to a certain number of pages not only lighten the reading burden for those making the selection, but also forces the audit firms to focus their response on the items specifically required by the request for proposal.

Finally, allow a reasonable time frame for the submission of the proposals, such as over a three- or four-week period. But also establish a specific deadline and refuse to consider proposals received after the deadline, unless there are extraordinary extenuating circumstances beyond the control of the proposing audit firm.

Determining Distribution of the Request for Proposal

Addressing this issue will vary depending on the state and locality in which the not-for-profit organization is based, as there are only a limited number of national audit firms, along with many regional and local firms. Judgment will have to be used to gauge the number of requests to distribute because receiving any more than 10 proposals will likely result in an unnecessary administrative burden. The audit committee also should consider whether to include national firms, regional firms, or local firms. This will be based in large part on the size of the not-for-profit organization. Midsize to larger organizations may choose to send requests for proposals to a cross section of these firms to assist in making comparisons to determine which type of firm would be best suited to audit the particular organization.

Disseminating Information to Proposers

In order for audit firms to prepare intelligent proposals, they will need information about the not-for-profit organization they are being asked to audit. Clearly, copies of the most recent audited financial statements should be made available to prospective proposers. The not-for-profit organization should also consider holding an information session for prospective proposers, during which that they can learn about the not-for-profit organization. Geographical dispersion of the organization's operating units, computer capabilities, centralization and location of accounting records, quality of internal accounting staff, and other factors can all have an impact on the fee estimates provided by firms, so it is to their advantage to find out as much about the organization prior to preparing their proposals.

Evaluating the Written Proposals

Since the audit committee is likely to be composed of approximately three to five members, it is usually practical to have all members participate on the selection team. In addition, because management will have day-to-day responsibilities for dealing with the auditor during the course of the audit, there is nothing inherently wrong with having them participate in the evaluation process as well. If the audit committee would like to maintain total control over the voting and ultimate selection of the new auditor, those in management could be made nonvoting members of the selection team. Not only will management be able to instruct staff members to summarize the proposals received, to make the audit committee's task easier, but they can also offer valuable insight into past successes and failures in dealing with independent auditors, insight the audit committee members would benefit from during the selection process.

One of the purposes of reviewing the written proposals is to determine which of the proposers should be invited to make an oral presentation to the selection committee about their qualifications, and to answer any questions that the selection committee may have. It is usually best to limit the number of invited audit firms for this purpose to three to five. This would make up an organization's short list of the firms best suited to it, based upon the evaluation of the written proposals.

Evaluating the Oral Presentations of Short-Listed Audit Firms

It is best to schedule the audit firms invited to make oral presentations to the selection committee members on the same day, if at all practical. Ideally, these presentations will last about half an hour, with an additional half-hour allowed for responding to questions of the selection committee members. It is very important that the audit firms be instructed to have those individuals who will be assigned to the audit at the partner and manager level make the presentation. One of the main purposes of the oral presentation is to meet and get to know the individuals who will be assigned to the account. Often audit firms will bring to the oral presentation a high-level partner at the audit firm (such as the firm's managing partner, at local or regional firms, or the managing partner of the office that will handle the audit, at larger firms) to demonstrate to the selection committee the importance of winning the contract to perform the not-for-profit organization's audit. Certainly, this is a nice gesture, but the audit committee members should keep in mind that they may never see this person again. What is important is that audit committee members get to know the partner and manager who will actually be handling the audit and interacting with the audit committee on a regular basis.

You may be thinking that the personalities of the audit partner and manager are being given too much consideration in the evaluation process. Make no mistake: The experience, reputation, commitment, and fees of the proposing firms are all very important factors to consider in the evaluation of the audit firms. However, it is the experience, reputation, and commitment of the actual individuals assigned to handle the audit that will matter most to the not-for-profit organization. In addition, as will be seen later in this chapter and the next, the audit committee will have significant dealings with the independent auditor. Therefore, they need to feel comfortable in their communications with the audit firm, specifically with the audit partner and manager handling the not-for-profit organization's audit. Thus, the audit committee members should be evaluating whether these individuals seem capable of providing them with open, objective, and sound information resulting from their audit.

Completing the Evaluation Process and Selecting the Auditor

Ideally, at the conclusion of the oral presentations, the audit committee members will have enough information enabling them to "vote" and select the independent auditor for the not-for-profit organization. Sometimes, some of the presenting audit firms may be asked to clarify certain information in their proposals and to provide additional information to the selection committee at a later date. Sometimes the selection committee may seek to either lower fees or obtain some other type of concession from the audit firms by requesting "best and final" offers, meaning that the audit firms are given the opportunity to update and resubmit their proposals based upon what they have learned from the evaluation process. All of these circumstances are really too specific to the individual selections to cover in depth here, but audit committee members should at least be aware that such processes exist, so that they can consider whether they need to use them.

Using an Audit Firm's Report as Part of the Evaluation Process

One of the documents that the preceding discussion suggested that proposing audit firms provide to the not-for-profit organization is a peer review report. Many audit committee members may be unfamiliar with this report, so this section provides some background information on it so that they will know how to use it in the proper context.

Most independent auditors undergo a review of their accounting and auditing practice at least once every three years. The independent audit firm hires another independent audit firm to perform the review—which is why it's called a peer review. The reviewing audit firm must be independent of the audit firm that it is the subject of the review and must be qualified to perform the review.

A peer review assists an audit committee in assessing whether the audit firm it is considering hiring:

- Has a system of quality control for its accounting and auditing practice that is designed to meet the requirements of the American Institute of Certified Public Accountant's (AICPA's) Statements on Quality Control Standards (SQCSs).
- Has complied with that quality control system during the peer review year, which provides the audit firm with reasonable assurance that it is complying with professional standards.

The AICPA's quality control standards provide requirements in various areas, such as:

- The auditor's independence, integrity, and objectivity
- Audit personnel management
- Acceptance and continuance of audit clients and engagements
- Audit engagement performance
- Firmwide quality control monitoring

There are three difference types of peer review reports. These are as follows:

1. *Unmodified report.* This report indicates that the audit firm's system of quality control has been designed to meet the requirements of the quality control standards for an accounting and auditing practice, and that the system was being complied with during the peer review year, in order to provide the audit firm with reasonable assurance of compliance with professional standards.
2. *Modified report.* This report indicates that the design of the audit firm's system of quality control created a condition in which the audit firm did not have reasonable assurance of complying with professional standards, or that the audit firm's degree of compliance with its quality control policies and procedures did not provide it with reasonable assurance of complying with professional standards.
3. *Adverse report.* This report means that there are significant deficiencies in the design of the audit firm's system of quality control, pervasive instances of non-compliance with the system as a whole, or both, resulting in several material failures to adhere to professional standards on engagements.

Both unmodified and modified reports are typically accompanied by a letter of comments. A letter of comments describes matters that the audit firm performing the period review believes resulted in conditions causing more than a remote possibility that the audit firm being reviewed would not comply with professional standards. The letter of comments includes recommendations regarding these matters.

A letter of comments is not prepared when an adverse report is issued because the deficiencies, comments, and recommendations would be included in the peer review report itself. The audit firm under review is required to respond in writing to the comments in the letter of comments.

The audit committee should obtain a copy of the most recent peer review report, along with the letter of comments and the reviewed audit firm's responses. The comments noted in these documents should be discussed with any prospective new auditor.

UNDERSTANDING THE INDEPENDENT
AUDIT OF FINANCIAL STATEMENTS

To effectively serve as an audit committee member, an individual does not need in-depth knowledge of how audits of financial statements are performed, but a general understanding of the types of procedures that independent auditors are (and are not) performing can help an audit committee member more effectively use and interpret on the work of the independent auditor in fulfilling his or her responsibilities. Just as important, gaining this understanding prevents the audit committee member from unjustifiably relying too heavily on the work that the independent auditor is performing. Just as you don't need to know all of the details of how a car works in order to drive it, it does come in handy to at least know something of what is going on under the hood, so that you know, for example, whether you should immediately pull off the road when the "check engine" light comes on.

This section will provide a brief overview of the process generally used by independent auditors to perform an audit of financial statements. It will help audit committee members understand the audit plans and required communications received from independent auditors, which will be discussed in the next chapter. It will also help audit committee members to interpret the various types of audit reports that can be issued on the financial statements by the independent auditor.

The following are the basic steps an auditor uses in auditing financial statements:

1. Plan the audit.
2. Consider internal control.
3. Perform substantive tests of financial statement balances.
4. Make conclusions based on the results of the audit procedures.
5. Perform general types of audit procedures.
6. Report on the results of the audit.

The following sections briefly describe what would be useful for audit committee members to understand about each of these activities.

Plan the Audit

The independent auditor begins the audit of the financial statements by planning the audit. This is the phase during which the auditor will determine the various different areas to which they will apply audit procedures. The auditor takes the important financial statement accounts and plans audit procedures to make sure that the relevant assertions inherent in each of these accounts is covered by the planned audit procedures.

One of the important aspects of the planning process for the auditor is to communicate with the audit committee for the purpose of determining whether committee members have any concerns and, if appropriate, to incorporate those concerns into the design of the audit strategy that will be used. The auditor should also discuss with the audit committee members whether they have any particular concerns regarding fraud and any fraud risk factors that the auditor should consider in the course of the audit.

The independent auditor will also perform preliminary analytical review procedures during the planning phase of the audit. These procedures are designed to determine whether the not-for-profit organization's preliminary financial information for the year makes sense when compared to other information, such as budgets and prior-year financial information. This activity is intended to help the auditor direct his or her attention to areas that might be of concern. For example, if an auditor sees that a particular expense is far under budget, he or she might focus certain audit procedures on that expense to determine whether there are any unrecorded expenses. Likewise, if the auditor notes that the contributions receivable account has grown significantly from the prior year, he or she will focus specific audit procedures on that area to determine whether the additional receivables recorded are valid or that, perhaps, a collectibility problem has arisen—say, that contributions receivable are not being collected on a timely basis.

The other notable step that an auditor takes during the planning phase of the audit is to determine a level of *materiality* to use in designing audit tests and concluding on audit results. Materiality is defined in the auditing standards as "the magnitude of an omission or misstatement of accounting information that, in light of surrounding circumstances, makes it probable that the judgment of a reasonable person relying on the information would have been changed or influenced by the omission or misstatement." In other words, an item is considered material if it would have an effect on the reader of the financial statements. The lower the level of materiality, the more audit test work the auditor will perform. The higher the level of materiality, the less audit test work the auditor will perform.

Finally, the auditor will map out an audit strategy to determine how much testing of internal control and financial statement balances to perform in order to form an opinion on the financial statements as a whole. Both of these areas will be described in the next two sections.

Consider Internal Control

An extensive discussion of internal control was provided in Chapter 4 of this book, so this section focuses only on the auditor's consideration of internal control. Contrary to popular opinion, auditors are not required to perform tests on a not-for-profit organization's internal control system. The auditor is required only to consider the not-for-profit organization's internal control system and incorporate its conclusions into the final audit strategy. In the past, this consideration was called the "determination" of whether the auditor could "rely" on an organization's internal controls (thus reducing the amount of other audit tests necessary to perform) or could not or chose not to rely on the internal controls. The current terminology for reliance on internal control is assessing control risk below the maximum level, which is a bit confusing. Control risk is the risk that an error or fraud occurs and is not prevented or detected by the internal control system on a timely basis. To assess control risk at the maximum level, the auditor has to decide that either the internal controls over financial reporting are not effective or that, from an efficiency perspective, the auditor is better off not testing internal controls, instead doing more of the substantive tests of financial statement balances, which will be described shortly. If an auditor decides to assess control risk at below the maximum level (that is, at low level or some other midpoint), the auditor would have to perform some tests of internal controls to validate his or her assumption that the risk of the internal control system not preventing or detecting an error or fraud is less than the maximum level. Note that, in this case, if the auditor does test internal controls over financial reporting and does find errors that lead him or her to conclude that control risk is at the maximum level, the auditor is back to square one and will have to perform more substantive tests of financial statement balances than originally planned.

What is important for an audit committee member to understand is that if the auditor believes that the not-for-profit organization's internal controls are not well designed or are not operating as designed, the auditor does not have to test the internal control. Likewise, if the auditor believes that it is more efficient not to test internal controls, the auditor may elect not to do so, even if the internal controls are properly designed and likely to be operating as designed. In both of these cases, the auditor would have to do more substantive tests of balances that are reported on the statement of net assets and statement of activities of the not-for-profit organization.

In addition, comments about an organization's internal control system that are noted in the letter of recommendations to management are based only on the auditor's consideration of that system, regardless of whether the auditor actually tested controls. Accordingly, audit committee members should not view the management letter as necessarily being the result of an extensive evaluation and testing of internal controls. It is merely a by-product of the audit designed to form an opinion on the financial statements; it is not designed to find internal control deficiencies.

Perform Substantive Tests of Financial Statement Balances

As just stated, auditors do not have to perform detailed tests of internal control, but they wouldn't be able to form an opinion on the financial statements without performing tests of balances and amounts that are recorded in the financial statements.

These tests are called "substantive" because they test balances. (Tests of internal controls are called "compliance" tests because they test compliance with the internal control system.) Substantive tests are conducted to, for example:

- Confirm bank account balances by the auditor directly with the bank.
- Confirm contributions receivable by the auditor directly with the donor (or determine that the receivable was collected after year-end).
- Review additions to fixed assets to make sure the items should have been capitalized and not expensed.
- Observe the physical counting of inventory at the end of the fiscal year.
- Search for unrecorded liabilities by reviewing disbursements made after year-end to see if any of these expenses should have been accrued back to the year being audited.
- Scan statements from the not-for-profit organization's vendors to make sure that no large unpaid balances go unrecorded in the accounting system.
- Verify the calculation of other large liabilities, such as the estimated amounts payable for litigation or disallowances of costs that have been charged to cost-reimbursable grant programs.
- Perform analytical procedures to obtain evidence that the financial statement amounts "make sense" in relation to each other, as well as to other quantifiable measures. For example, by multiplying the number of employees of the not-for-profit organization by an estimate of the average salary of an employee, the independent auditor can calculate an expectation of what the payroll expense would be and then compare this expectation to what is actually recorded in the financial statements.

The auditor uses an appropriate mix of these types of audit procedures to make sure that he or she is covering all of the significant assertions about financial statement amounts that are inherent in those amounts. Note that when performing audit procedures in one area, the auditor will obtain audit evidence about other audit areas. For example, in auditing contributions receivable from donors, the auditor is also obtaining evidence about the contribution revenue that is recorded in the statement of activities in the financial statements.

Perform General Types of Audit Procedures

Other audit procedures that auditors perform are more general in nature as compared to a detailed test of a financial statement account balance. For example, the auditor should send inquiry letters to any lawyers who advise the not-for-profit organization, to learn whether there is any existing or threatened litigation against the organization. If so, the lawyer is asked to make an assessment of the likelihood of financial exposure to the not-for-profit organization, and the dollar amount of that exposure. In this way the auditor obtains evidence as to whether appropriate litigation liabilities are recorded in the financial statements and whether any required disclosures are made in the notes to the financial statements.

Auditors will also obtain a representation letter from management in which the chief executive and chief financial officers of the organization confirm in writing to the independent auditors a number of different things, but primarily that the financial statements of the not-for-profit organization are presented in conformity with generally accepted accounting principles. The representation letter also lists many specific areas in which management confirms whether there are matters related to these areas. For example, management confirms to the independent auditor whether there are unasserted legal claims against the not-for-profit organization.

Make Conclusions Based on the Results of Audit Procedures

As audit procedures are being performed, the independent auditor keeps a scorecard of what are commonly called "audit differences." These are differences between what the auditor believes a financial statement account or balance should be and what is actually being reported on the financial statements. It's important for audit committee members to understand what these audit differences represent, as the independent auditor will be discussing these with them.

Some audit differences are "hard" (known differences) and some are "soft" (likely). For example, an auditor selects individual donor contributions receivable totaling $10,000 out of a total financial statement balance of $100,000 in this category. Of the sampled items, the auditor determines that $1,000 is overstated because one donor contribution receivable was recorded twice, in error. Thus the auditor has a known audit difference of $1,000. However, the auditor must also address the fact that 10 percent ($1,000 out of $10,000) of his or her sample was overstated, so there is a possibility that 10 percent of all the contributions may be overstated. So, 10 percent of $100,000 minus $10,000 is the total projected misstatement of this account, of which $1,000 is an actual difference; and the balance, $9,000 is the projected difference. The $9,000 is a projected likely audit difference because it represents an estimation of the potential misstatement based upon the sample.

The auditor accumulates all of the audit differences, as just described, and determines whether these differences, both individually and in the aggregate, cause a material misstatement of the financial statements. In practice, the independent auditor reviews these adjustments with the management of the not-for-profit organization, which may decide to record some or all of the adjustments in the financial statements. Accordingly then, the auditor would need to determine whether the unrecorded audit differences, both individually and in the aggregate, result in a material misstatement of the financial statements. If they do not cause a material misstatement of the financial statements, the auditor can issue an "unqualified" opinion on the financial statements, but must inform the audit committee of any audit differences that were not recorded by management. If the unrecorded adjustments do cause a material misstatement of the financial statements, and management refuses to record the adjustments, the auditor cannot issue an unqualified opinion on the financial statements, as is discussed next.

Report the Results of the Audit

The result of an independent audit of an organization's financial statements is the issuance of an opinion by the independent auditor as to whether the financial statements are presented in accordance with generally accepted accounting principles. Ideally, the audit committee will be reading an "unqualified" opinion on the financial statements; however, there are several variations of this opinion that may be rendered by the independent auditor, so audit committee members should have a general understanding of them, as well. Accordingly, this section presents a brief overview of these types of opinions:

- *Unqualified opinion.* Sometimes called a "clean" opinion, this is issued when the auditor concludes that the financial statements are fairly presented, in all material respects, in accordance with generally accepted accounting principles. The independent auditor has concluded that any unrecorded audit adjustments, if any, do not result in a material misstatement of the financial statements and that disclosures in the notes to the financial statements contain all of the disclosures for the particular organization that would be required by generally accepted accounting principles.

- *Qualified for a departure from generally accepted accounting principles.* This opinion states that the financial statements of the organization are presented in accordance with GAAP, "except for" one or more particular matters, which are then described by the auditor. For whatever reason, the not-for-profit organization has not followed generally accepted accounting principles for the item or items noted, and this is being reported to the reader by the independent auditor. For example, a not-for-profit organization may not have recorded a depreciation expense as required in the financial statements, resulting in an opinion qualification by the auditor.

- *Qualified opinion for an audit scope limitation.* This opinion is issued when an auditor cannot obtain sufficient audit evidence about a particular account balance or other element in the financial statements. The independent auditor's opinion is "subject to" any adjustments of the financial statements that would have been discovered had the auditor been able to complete his or her audit procedures for this particular item. For example, for a newly audited organization, an auditor would not be able to physically observe the counting of significant amounts of inventory as of the beginning of the fiscal year being audited, if the auditor was hired subsequent to the beginning of the fiscal year. If the auditor was unable to satisfy himself or herself as to the beginning-of-the-year balance with alternative procedures, a qualified opinion noting this audit scope limitation would be issued.

- *Adverse opinion.* An adverse opinion is issued when a departure from GAAP is so pervasive to the financial statements that the auditor has concluded the financial statements as a whole cannot be viewed as being prepared in accordance with GAAP. In other words, this opinion would be used as a more severe version of the "except for" qualified opinion described in the previous item.

- *Disclaimer of opinion.* Not really an opinion, this is a report in which the auditor states that he or she is unable to render an opinion on the financial statements as a whole. In other words, this nonopinion would be used as a more severe version of the "subject to" qualified opinion just described.

In addition to these opinions, there are several other reports and opinions that audit committee members may have to read. Here are some examples:

- For not-for-profit organizations that are recipients of federal awards programs and are subject to the Single Audit Act, the auditor will issue an opinion on the not-for-profit organization's compliance with program requirements for each of the organization's major federal programs, as well as a report on the internal controls related to compliance with these programs.
- For not-for-profit organizations requiring an audit to be performed in accordance with the *Government Auditing Standards* issued by the Comptroller General of the United States of America (which automatically includes those organizations required to have a Single Audit performed) the independent auditor will report on compliance with laws and regulations and internal controls at the financial statement level.
- Independent auditors also may issue opinions of financial statements prepared on certain comprehensive bases of accounting other than generally accepted accounting principles, such as the cash basis of accounting.

MONITORING THE INDEPENDENCE
OF THE INDEPENDENT AUDITOR

Independent auditors are subject to various requirements relating to independence. For example, a partner of an independent auditor generally would be seen as having his or her independence impaired with respect to a not-for-profit organization if he or she was also a member of the governing board of the organization. The most recent area of concern relating to independence, however, is the one that the audit committee will most likely have to understand and address regarding the independent auditor of a not-for-profit organization. The term "nonattest" is used to refer to services that include nonaudit services. Attest services include both audits and a type of engagement known as an *attestation engagement*. This area involves whether the performance of nonattest services by the independent auditor for the not-for-profit organization would impair the auditor's independence with respect to the organization. This section will focus on this area to assist audit committee members in developing best practices relating to whether the independent auditor is engaged to perform nonattest services.

There are a number of different sources of requirements for independence of independent auditors. Independent auditors performing audits of not-for-profit organizations should comply with the independence requirements of the American Institute of Certified Public Accountants (AICPA). The AICPA has recently issued an interpretation of its rules regarding the performance of nonattest services in Interpretation 101-3, "Performance of Nonattest Services." Audits of financial statements where compliance with the *Government Auditing Standards* apply (such as when a Single Audit is performed) need to comply with those standards' independence requirements. Further, for public companies, the Sarbanes-Oxley Act addresses the area of the performance of nonattest services, and the United States Securities and Exchange Commission invokes independence rules that implement the Sarbanes-Oxley Act requirements.

This section will provide an overview of the AICPA requirements to help audit committee members evaluate whether a particular nonattest service impairs the auditor's independence. Of course, it is the independent auditor who is primarily responsible for maintaining his or her independence, but as will be discussed shortly, an aspect of the requirements is to inform the audit committee about such services. This communication must be understood by the audit committee members so that they can be confident that the auditor's independence wouldn't be impaired by performing the services. The nonattest services requirements from the Sarbanes-Oxley Act as to independence will also be addressed so that audit committee members can decide whether they want to enforce the more restrictive features of these requirements.

AICPA Interpretation Regarding Performance of Nonattest Services

These requirements are described as follows:

- The independent auditor should not perform management functions or make management decisions for the client organization. However, the independent auditor may provide advice, research materials, and recommendations to assist management in performing its functions and making decisions.
- The client organization must agree to perform the following functions in connection with the engagement to perform nonattest services:
  - Make all management decisions and perform all management functions.
  - Designate an individual who possesses suitable skill, knowledge, and/or experience, preferably within senior management, to oversee the services.
  - Evaluate the adequacy and results of the services performed.
  - Accept responsibility for the results of the services.
  - Establish and maintain internal controls, including monitoring ongoing activities.
- Before performing nonattest services, the independent auditor should establish and document in writing his or her understanding with the client (governing board, audit committee, or management, as is appropriate) regarding the following:
  - Objectives of the engagement
  - Services to be performed
  - Client organization's acceptance of its responsibilities

- Independent auditor's responsibilities
- Any limitations on the engagement

The AICPA requirements specify that the second and third items above do not apply to certain routine activities performed by the independent auditor, such as providing advice and responding to the client organization's questions as part of the normal client-independent auditor relationship. The AICPA requirements also list some general activities that would impair an independent auditor's independence:

- Authorizing, executing, or consummating a transaction, or otherwise exercising authority on behalf of a client or having the authority to do so.
- Preparing source documents, in electronic or other form, evidencing the occurrence of a transaction.
- Having custody of client assets.
- Supervising client employees in the performance of their normal recurring activities.
- Determining which recommendations of the independent auditor should be implemented.
- Reporting to the governing board on behalf of management.
- Serving as a client's stock transfer or escrow agent, registrar, general counsel or its equivalent.

As can be discerned from these general principles and the specific example, the AICPA's requirements as to nonattest services focus on making sure that the management of the organization accepts and maintains responsibility for the nonattest engagement. Independent auditors cannot assume roles that are management in nature without impairing their independence.

Government Auditing Standards Independence Requirements

Several years ago, the Government Accountability Office (GAO—at the time, called the General Accounting Office) issued independence guidance for independent auditors performing nonaudit services. Because this guidance predated the AICPA revised guidance just described, this was a significantly new set of requirements that auditors had to comply with as to independence when performing audits in accordance with *Government Auditing Standards*. With the issuance of the AICPA requirements, the differences between the two requirements narrowed.

The GAO requirements as to the effect of performing nonaudit services on auditor independence are based on two overarching principles:

1. Audit organizations should not provide audit services that involve performing management functions or making management decisions.

2. Audit organizations should not audit their own work or provide nonaudit services in situations where the nonaudit services are significant/material to the subject matter of the audits.

If the audit organization determines that the nonaudit service does not violate these principles, the GAO specifies certain safeguards that should be put into place to ensure that the performance of the service does not impair auditor independence.

Sarbanes-Oxley Act Independence Requirements

The Sarbanes-Oxley Act independence requirements are contained in Section 201 of the act, "Services Outside the Scope of Practice of Auditors; Prohibited Activities." It provides (with certain exceptions discussed shortly) that it would be unlawful for an independent auditor to provide any nonaudit service to a public company covered by the act contemporaneously with the audit, including the following services specifically listed:

- Bookkeeping or other services related to the accounting records or financial statements of the audit client
- Financial information system design and implementation
- Appraisal or valuation services, fairness opinions, or contribution-in-kind reports
- Actuarial services
- Internal audit outsourcing services
- Management functions or human resources
- Broker or dealer, investment advisor, or investment banking services
- Legal services and expert services unrelated to the audit
- Any other service that the Public Company Accounting Oversight Board (PCAOB) determines, by regulation, is impermissible

The Sarbanes-Oxley Act provides that the PCAOB may, on a case-by-case basis, exempt from these provisions any person, public company issuer, public accounting firm, or transaction, subject to the review of the United States Securities and Exchange Commission.

The Sarbanes-Oxley Act allows an accounting firm to engage in any nonaudit service, including tax services that are not listed here, only if the activity is preapproved by the audit committee of the public company issuer. Further, this preapproval requirement is waived with respect to the provision of nonaudit services for a public company issuer if the aggregate amount of all such nonaudit services provided to the public company issuer constitutes less than 5 percent of the total amount of revenues paid by the public company issuer to its auditor, provided that such services were not recognized by the public company issuer at the time of the engagement to be nonaudit services and such services are promptly brought to the attention of the audit committee and approved prior to the completion of the audit.

Accordingly, the Sarbanes-Oxley Act essentially requires that only nonaudit services not prohibited can be performed by the independent auditor as long as the audit committee approves the use of the independent auditor to perform nonaudit services.

The choice for not-for-profit organizations is really to decide whether to apply the Sarbanes-Oxley requirements. The independent auditor will already need to comply with the AICPA requirements and, where a Single Audit is required, with the independence requirements of the *Government Auditing Standards*. However, there is really no need to establish a policy that restricts the use of the independent auditor to specific types of nonattest services, provided that the audit committee is required to approve any use of the independent auditor to provide nonattest services. The audit committee can then use the prohibited services listed here as a guide in evaluating specific projects presented to it, considering the size and scope of the nonattest services to be performed, in order to reach a decision as to whether to approve the nonattest services to be provided by the independent auditor.

BEST PRACTICE

The audit committee of the not-for-profit organization should preapprove any nonattest services proposed to be performed by the organization's independent auditor.

One other factor to keep in mind is that many smaller not-for-profit organizations that do not have large accounting staffs often rely on the independent auditor to prepare and record year-end closing accounting entries, as well as to draft the financial statements. The audit committee should gain an understanding of the extent to which management takes responsibility for recording all accounting transactions, including year-end closing accounting entries, as well as drafting the financial statements, so that they can be confident that the auditor's independence is not being impaired.

COMMUNICATIONS RECEIVED FROM
THE INDEPENDENT AUDITOR

Generally accepted auditing standards require that independent auditors communicate certain information to audit committees. These requirements apply to all audits performed in accordance with generally accepted auditing standards, which include audits of not-for-profit organizations. The basic requirements of these communications are set forth in the Statement on Auditing Standards No. 61, "Communication with Audit Committees," which independent auditors often refer to as the "SAS-61" report.

Auditors have the option of providing this information either orally or in writing to the audit committee, meaning that audit committees won't always receive this information in a document. Some of these matters may have been reported to the audit committee already by management (such as a change in an accounting policy). In these cases, the auditor does not have to repeat the information to the audit committee, but must make sure that it has in fact been communicated to the audit committee.

The following is a brief overview of the required communications, along with explanations, to better enable audit committee members to understand this information.

Auditor's Responsibilities under Generally Accepted Auditing Standards

This section of the SAS-61 report requires that the independent auditor explain to the audit committee his or her level of responsibility when issuing an opinion that the financial statements of the not-for-profit organization are free of material misstatement. The independent auditor will inform the audit committee that an audit conducted in accordance with generally accepted auditing standards is designed to provide reasonable, as opposed to absolute, assurance as to the financial statements. Audit committee members who have read this far in this book will have a very good understanding of the nature and limitations of an audit performed in accordance with generally accepted auditing standards.

Summary of Significant Accounting Policies

The auditor is required to ensure that the audit committee is informed about the initial selection of and changes in significant accounting policies or the application of these policies. The audit committee must also be informed about the methods used to account for significant unusual transactions and the effect of significant accounting policies in controversial or emerging areas for which there is a lack of authoritative guidance or consensus. Audit committee members should understand that there are instances where different ways to account for certain transactions or events exist, and the organization will select which accounting policy it will use in the financial statements. Sometimes organizations will change an accounting policy that it uses for certain transactions or events. Audit committee members should be familiar with the accounting policies and the application of these policies and any changes made by the organization from year to year. In addition, there may be unusual events or transactions for which the proper accounting may be unclear, or is the result of a selection from alternatives. Audit committees should understand when these circumstances exist and be comfortable with the accounting methods selected.

Note that a subsequent auditing standard amended the requirements of SAS-61 for audits of public companies, to include information about the independent auditor's judgments about the quality of an organization's accounting principles. These requirements are discussed later in this chapter.

Management Judgments and Accounting Estimates

Accounting estimates, an integral part of the financial statements, are based upon the current judgments of management. For example, a not-for-profit organization may have an allowance for uncollectible pledges receivable, which represents an estimate of the pledges receivable that it has recorded as an asset that will not be ultimately collected. These types of estimates are based on knowledge and experience about past and current events and on assumptions about future events. Certain accounting estimates are particularly sensitive because of their significance to the financial statements and because of the possibility that future events affecting them may differ markedly from management's current judgments.

The independent auditor is required to determine that the audit committee is informed about: (1) the process used by management in formulating particularly sensitive accounting estimates and (2) the basis for the auditor's conclusions regarding the reasonableness of those estimates. Estimates often encountered in financial statements include those related to pension and other-than-pension postemployment benefits and liabilities resulting from litigation or environmental remediation liabilities. Audit committee members need to be aware that the financial statements contain a number of very important estimates; furthermore, they should be satisfied that management has made these estimates using the best possible information available and that the independent auditor has concluded that the estimates being used in the financial statements are reasonable.

Audit Adjustments

Independent auditors are required to inform the audit committee about adjustments to the financial statements arising from the audit that could, in the independent auditor's judgment, have a significant effect on the organization's financial reporting process when the adjustments are considered either individually or in the aggregate. An audit adjustment is a proposed correction of the financial statements that, in the independent auditor's judgment, may not have been detected except through the auditing procedures performed. Note that audit adjustments may or may not have been recorded by the organization in the financial statements. For adjustments that have been recorded, the auditor is required to inform the audit committee about these adjustments if they are considered to have had a significant effect on the organization's financial reporting process. Basically, the independent auditor is required to inform the audit committee about significant audit adjustments that were recorded by management in the financial statements.

For audit adjustments that have not been recorded by management in the financial statements, the requirements are a little different. The independent auditor is required to inform the audit committee about uncorrected misstatements (i.e., unrecorded audit adjustments) aggregated by the independent auditor during the current year's audit that were determined by the management of the not-for-profit organization to be immaterial to the financial statements as a whole, when considering those misstatements either individually or in the aggregate. Basically, the audit committee must be informed as to the effect of all unrecorded audit adjustments on the not-for-profit organization's financial statements.

Audit committee members should view these two pieces of information differently, as follows:

1. If significant audit adjustments were identified by the auditor and recorded by management, the audit committee member may question what is faulty in the financial reporting process of the organization, necessitating significant adjustments to the financial statements by the auditor. In short, why can't the organization prepare financial statements that don't require significant adjustments by the auditor?
2. If there are unrecorded audit differences, the audit committee member should be comfortable with the decision of management to not record these adjustments in the financial statements. The independent auditor will be careful to state that it is management that has determined the unrecorded audit adjustments do not have a material effect on the financial statements; nevertheless, the auditor is implicitly concurring with this judgment, assuming he or she will be issuing an unqualified opinion on the financial statements. Audit committee members may find it helpful to ask why management did not record the audit adjustments in the financial statements. In some cases management may feel the unrecorded audit adjustments are far to small to even approach having a material effect on the financial statements. In other cases, management and the independent auditor may have arrived at an amount in the financial statements (particularly in the case of estimates) that is different from what the auditor arrived at through independent calculation, but management doesn't believe that the auditor's amount is any better than the one they calculated, and so declines to record the difference between the two as an adjustment.

Auditor's Judgments about the Quality of the Organization's Accounting Principles

As noted earlier, this requirement applies to audits of public companies, although the independent auditor may voluntarily communicate this information to audit committees of not-for-profit organizations. Indeed, the audit committee of a not-for-profit organization may specifically request the auditor to address these issues, even though the discussion is not required by generally accepted auditing standards for audits of these types of organizations.

This requirement obliges the independent auditor to discuss with the audit committee the independent auditor's judgments about the quality, not just the acceptability, of an organization's accounting principles as applied in its financial reporting. The auditing standard notes that, because management is responsible for establishing an organization's accounting principles, this discussion would include management as an active participant. The discussion should be open and frank and include such matters as the consistency of the organization's accounting policies and their application, and the clarity and completeness of the organization's financial statements, including the related disclosures. The discussion should also include items that have a significant impact on the representational faithfulness, verifiability, and neutrality of the accounting information included in the financial statements. In other words: Do the financial statements do a good job of presenting the financial position and activities of the not-for-profit organization? Can the auditor readily verify information in the financial statements? And are the financial statements free of a bias toward overly aggressive or overly conservative accounting treatments of events and transactions? Examples of items that may have an impact on these areas provided include:

- Selection of new or changes to accounting policies
- Estimates, judgments, and uncertainties
- Unusual transactions
- Accounting policies relating to significant financial statement items, including the timing of transactions and the period in which they are recorded

The discussion should be tailored to the organization's specific circumstances, including accounting applications and practices not explicitly addressed in the accounting literature, such as those that might be specific to the not-for-profit industry.

Audit committee members may help the voluntary compliance with these requirements by an independent auditor of a not-for-profit organization to be very useful in assessing the overall selection and application of accounting principles by the not-for-profit organization. Instead of addressing the appropriateness of each individual accounting policy or application that is employed in the financial statements, the discussion described here seeks to determine whether management and the independent auditor believe that, taken as a whole, the application of all accounting policies result in financial statements that appropriately portray the financial position and activities of the organization.

Other Information in Documents Containing Audited Financial Statements

The auditor is required to discuss with the audit committee his or her responsibility for other information in documents that contain the audited financial statements. For example, the not-for-profit organization may produce a "glossy" annual report that provides a summary of the organization's activities for the year and that includes the audited financial statements. The independent auditor should describe to the audit committee his or her responsibility for the information in the annual report that is accompanied by the audited financial statements. The independent auditor's basic responsibility is to read the accompanying information and make sure that there is nothing in it that is inconsistent with the audited financial statements.

Disagreements with Management

Disagreements between the independent auditor and management may occasionally occur over the application of accounting principles to the not-for-profit organization's specific transactions and events, and the basis for management's judgments about accounting estimates. Disagreements may also arise regarding the scope of the audit, disclosures to be included in the organization's financial statements, and the wording of the auditor's report. The independent auditor should discuss with the audit committee any disagreements with management, whether or not satisfactorily resolved, regarding matters that individually or in the aggregate could be significant to the organization's financial statements or the auditor's report. For the purpose of these requirements, disagreements do not include differences of opinion based on incomplete facts or preliminary information that are later resolved.

Clearly, the audit committee would be interested in any disagreements between management and the independent auditor, with an eye toward understanding how the differences were resolved in the financial statements. It's important to note that this requirement relates even to those disagreements that have been resolved. Independent auditors are likely to be reluctant to discuss disagreements that are ultimately resolved to both parties' satisfaction, hence may tend to use the "incomplete information exception" as a way to avoid bringing a resolved disagreement to the audit committee's attention. Audit committee members may find it useful to ask some probing questions related to any potential disagreements, which may result in more information about resolved disagreements being brought forth with the audit committee members.

Consultation with Other Accountants

Management may decide to consult with other accountants about auditing and accounting matters. When the independent auditor of the not-for-profit organization is aware that such consultation has occurred, he or she should discuss with the audit committee his or her views about significant matters that were the subject of such consultations.

The audit committee should be aware of any "opinion shopping" by management. For example, if management seeks to account for a specific transaction in some particular way, they might contact another audit firm and inquire as to whether management's proposed accounting treatment of the transaction would be acceptable under generally accepted accounting principles. If this other audit firm agrees with management's accounting treatment, management can use this agreement as leverage with the not-for-profit organization's independent auditor in applying the accounting treatment for the transaction that is desired by management. While there may be nothing wrong with the accounting treatment being proposed by management in this example, the audit committee should certainly be on the lookout for any perceived "bullying" of the organization's independent auditor by using the opinion of another audit firm.

Major Issues Discussed with Management Prior to Retention

The independent auditor is required to discuss with the audit committee any major issues that were addressed with management in connection with the initial or recurring retention of the independent auditor, including any discussions regarding the application of accounting principles and auditing standards. The underlying principle that would make such discussions of interest to the audit committee is that the decision to hire or retain an independent should not be contingent in any way upon their agreeing to a specific accounting treatment or application of auditing standards. Clearly, if the audit committee manages the process for hiring the independent auditor, there might be less opportunity for such consultations. However, audit committee members should be alert to the existence of any preretention agreements as to accounting and/or audit matters. Thus, this requirement is meant to make the audit committee members aware when such discussions take place. This is not to imply, however, that such discussions automatically mean that some inappropriate agreement has taken place between management and the independent auditor. Rather, the requirement is simply a mechanism for putting the burden on the auditor to disclose any such discussions to the audit committee so that its members can be confident that any discussions were appropriate.

Difficulties Encountered in Performing the Audit

The independent auditor is required to inform the audit committee of any serious difficulties that were encountered in dealing with management during the performance of the audit. These serious difficulties may include, among others, unreasonable delays by management in permitting the commencement of the audit or in providing needed information, and whether the timetable set by management was unreasonable under the circumstances. Other matters that the independent auditor might encounter include the unavailability of client personnel and the failure of client personnel to complete client-prepared schedules on a timely basis. If the auditor considers these matters to be significant, he or she should inform the audit committee.

The first set of examples here, provided by SAS-61, can be read to imply an *intent* by management to severely limit the time available for the independent auditors to complete their work, ostensibly for the purpose of rushing their work so that their audit is less thorough. Obviously, if an independent auditor reports any such difficulties, the audit committee is being alerted to what may be a very serious problem regarding the integrity of management. In contrast, the second set of examples may be more circumstantial and less intentional on the part of management. For example, perhaps there was a dramatic turnover in accounting department personnel, resulting in the auditor receiving less help than expected from the not-for-profit organization's staff in performing and completing the audit. In such cases, the audit committee may be more concerned with whether the organization has adequate accounting resources to properly maintain its accounting records and controls, rather than as an intent on the part of management to make it as difficult as possible for the independent auditor to perform and complete the audit.

Required Communications Summary

In reading about the matters that an independent auditor is required to communicate to the audit committee, it should be obvious that the audit committee can learn very valuable information from the independent auditor as a result of these required communications. The audit committee should make it clear to the independent auditor that it values these communications and expects that the independent auditor will ensure that all required disclosures will be made to the audit committee. It's important to say this, because as has been observed in practice, the reporting under SAS-61 has become somewhat pro forma, with independent auditors sometimes rattling through a bulleted laundry list of these required communications, providing very little in the way of information to the audit committee. At the same time, many audit committee members might not really understand the nature and reason for these SAS-61 communications, and so may overlook their value. In these cases, the independent auditor is likely to communicate the bare minimum required, meaning the audit committee will not learn much.

A better approach would be to formalize the SAS-61 communications as a specific audit committee meeting agenda item, then allow sufficient time for the required items to be discussed. Audit committee members may find it useful to ask some probing questions of the independent auditor to encourage such discussions. For example, if no difficulties in performing the audit were communicated by the auditor, the audit committee members might ask if the audit began and ended on schedule, if all client-prepared schedules were received on a timely basis, and so on.

BEST PRACTICE

The audit committee of a not-for-profit organization should spend an appropriate amount of time with the independent auditor discussing the communications required by SAS-61. The committee should also recognize that these communications can be very valuable in helping members fulfill their responsibilities.

OPTIONAL ATTESTATION ABOUT MANAGEMENT'S ASSERTIONS REGARDING INTERNAL CONTROL OVER FINANCIAL REPORTING

In describing the activities of the independent auditor, the focus has been on the requirements of an independent auditor while performing an audit of financial statements in accordance with generally accepted auditing standards. An additional service that may also be requested of the independent auditor is to perform an audit of internal control over financial reporting, which is the basic requirement of Section 404 of the Sarbanes-Oxley Act. Here, too, compliance with this section would be a voluntary undertaking for not-for-profit organizations that are not subject to the requirements of the Sarbanes-Oxley Act. However, many not-for-profit organizations are considering whether some or all of the requirements of the Sarbanes-Oxley Act may be useful to adopt; and its requirement of independent auditors of financial statements to perform an audit of internal control over financial reporting and attest to management's assertions about these internal controls is certainly a major component of the act.

This section will briefly describe the work relating to internal control that independent auditors perform and that not-for-profit organizations and their audit committees may wish to consider as part of their audit process.

Attestation Standards of the American Institute of Certified Public Accountants

Many audit committee members may not realize that, long before the Sarbanes-Oxley Act was passed, independent auditors could be engaged to perform procedures and reach conclusions about internal controls over financial reporting. These engagements have been and continue to be covered by attestation standards issued by the American Institute of Certified Public Accountants (AICPA). Attestation standards are different from auditing standards in that the object is not an opinion on an organization's financial statements; rather, the practitioner (not referred to as an "auditor," as the procedures are not being performed under the auditing standards) "attests" to assertions made by another party (called the "responsible party"), which, in the case of internal controls over financial reporting, is basically management.

The practitioner's objective in an engagement to examine the effectiveness of an organization's internal control is to express an opinion on:

(a) the effectiveness of the organization's internal control, in all material respects, based on the control criteria, or
(b) whether the responsible party's written assertion about the effectiveness of internal control is fairly stated, in all material respects, based on the control criteria.

The opinion relates to the effectiveness of the organization's internal control taken as a whole, of each individual control component. (Remember from the chapter regarding internal control that the five components of internal control are: the control environment, risk assessment, control activities, information and communication, and monitoring.) The practitioner (1) considers the interrelationships of the components of the organization's internal control to meet the objective of the control criteria, and (2) accumulates sufficient evidence about the design effectiveness and operating effectiveness of the organization's internal control. The practitioner performing an examination as to the effectiveness of an organization's internal control will take the following broad steps:

1. Plan the engagement.
2. Obtain an understanding of internal control.
3. Evaluate the design effectiveness of the controls.
4. Test and evaluate the operating effectiveness of the controls.
5. Form an opinion on the effectiveness of the organization's internal control, or management's assertion thereon based on the control criteria.

Note that in conducting this examination, the practitioner needs to consider both whether the internal controls are designed to be effective and whether properly designed controls are operating effectively.

Audit committees may consider engaging the independent auditor in the role of "practitioner" to perform an attest function regarding internal control. This type of engagement is not unlike that described in the next section regarding the standards for public companies under the Sarbanes-Oxley Act, although the practitioner may be able to tailor the examination to meet the specific needs of the audit committee. For example, perhaps it would be more effective for the auditor (or other selected practitioner) to perform the attestation engagement regarding internal control separate from the audit of the financial statements. Also, the audit committee may find it useful to have the practitioner examine and attest to only certain aspects of the organization's internal control in any given year, perhaps setting up a rotation schedule for different financial reporting cycles (such as the revenue or expenditure cycle) so that the cost of the services each year can be minimized. To determine how to accomplish this for a particular not-for-profit organization, the audit committee should ask the independent auditor what options would be available if the audit committee decided to pursue this approach.

Audit of Internal Control over Financial Reporting Performed in Accordance with the Public Company Accounting Oversight Board Standards

The Sarbanes-Oxley Act transferred the responsibility for setting auditing standards for audits of public companies from the AICPA to a newly created organization, the Public Companies Accounting Oversight Board (PCAOB). One of the first moves the PCAOB made was to issue a new standard to guide auditors in their performance of audits of internal control over financial reporting as required by Section 404 of the Sarbanes-Oxley Act. In March 2004, the PCAOB issued Auditing Standard No. 2, "An Audit of Internal Control over Financial Reporting Performed in Conjunction with an Audit of Financial Statements" (AS-2).

The auditor's objective when conducting an audit of internal control over financial reporting under AS-2 is to express an opinion on management's assessment of the effectiveness of the organization's internal control over financial reporting. To form a basis for expressing such an opinion, the auditor must plan and perform the audit to obtain reasonable assurance as to whether the organization maintained, in all material respects, effective internal control over financial reporting as of the date specified in management's assessment.

Under AS-2 the auditor also must audit the organization's financial statements as of the date specified in management's assertions, because the information the auditor obtains during a financial statement audit is relevant to the auditor's conclusion about the effectiveness of the organization's internal control over financial reporting. Maintaining effective internal control over financial reporting is defined to mean that no material weaknesses exist. Accordingly, the objective of the audit of internal control over financial reporting under AS-2 is to obtain reasonable assurance that no material weaknesses exist as of the date specified in management's assessment.

In performing an audit of an organization's internal control over financial reporting, the following steps are involved:

1. Plan the engagement.
2. Evaluate management's assessment process.
3. Obtain an understanding of internal control over financial reporting.
4. Test and evaluate the design effectiveness of internal control over financial reporting.
5. Test and evaluate operating effectiveness of internal control over financial reporting.
6. Form an opinion on the effectiveness of internal control over financial reporting.

It may be difficult to distinguish in an overview such as this how AS-2 is different from the AICPA attestation engagement described in the preceding section. Defining the specific differences is beyond the scope of this book, but the audit committee member should understand that the AS-2 requirements for auditors performing and reporting on this type of audit are far more specific that those under the attestation standards. In addition, the audit of internal control over financial reporting under AS-2 is far more integrated into the audit of the financial statements, requiring that the same independent auditor who audits the financial statements also audit internal control. AS-2 also requires that the auditor evaluate management's assessment process; and it has more specific reporting requirements, including the expression of an opinion on the internal control over financial reporting.

In determining what, if any, additional procedures regarding internal control the audit committee requests of the "practitioner" or independent auditor under the AICPA attestation standards or the PCAOB requirements, the audit committee members should evaluate the benefits expected to be derived from enhancing their oversight of the financial reporting of the not-for-profit organization and to the organization itself, when compared with the costs of obtaining these services under either approach. The experience of public companies under Section 404 and AS-2 requirements has been that these types of audits of internal control require a significant amount of resources, both from in the form of organization staff's time and effort as well as in the remuneration of the independent auditor who performs these additional audit procedures.

SUMMARY

The relationship between audit committee members and an independent auditor is key to the successful fulfillment of the audit committee's responsibilities. Understanding the nature of an independent audit of financial statements and learning what additional procedures an independent auditor may be requested to perform are important steps in establishing best practices for the audit committee of any not-for-profit organization.

Chapter 8

An Audit Committee Action Plan

The preceding chapters of this book examined many issues and topics that not-for-profit organization audit committees must understand and evaluate—from basics of financial reporting to the audit committee and its operating rules to internal control to management's relationship with the organization's independent auditor. Now that these building blocks have been put in place, audit committee members are well equipped to effectively meet their responsibilities to the committee, the governing board, and the not-for-profit organization itself. This chapter will use all of these building blocks to develop a strategy that audit committees can use as a template for setting their annual workload. In other words, this chapter will describe how to put into action the knowledge that audit committee members have gained so far in this book. Whereas in previous chapters many specific action steps were discussed, which audit committees need to take in each area, this chapter will provide a road map for implementing all of those steps throughout the course of a financial reporting year.

Specifically, this chapter will discuss the agendas of each of the audit committee's most important meetings. These routine meetings include the following:

- Holding an organizational meeting.
- Reviewing the audit plan with the independent auditor.
- Reviewing the audit results and drafts of financial statements.
- Reviewing the independent auditor's management letter and addressing internal control issues.

In addition to these meetings, which should occur every fiscal year, there are additional meetings (or elements of meetings) that the audit committee should hold during the year or on an as-needed basis. These meetings are referred to as "executive sessions," and the content of these meetings will be discussed later in this chapter.

HOLDING AN ORGANIZATIONAL MEETING

Prior to the commencement of the audit committee's involvement with the audit of the not-for-profit organization's financial statements, it is recommended that the audit committee hold an organizational meeting to prepare for the upcoming audit committee year. The following topics should be considered for inclusion on the agenda for this meeting.

Attend to Committee Meeting Details

The attendance of all committee members at audit committee meetings is important to the success of the committee's actions, and by providing as much advance notice as possible to them, you improve the chances of their attendance. Accordingly, establishing meeting dates early (and avoiding rescheduling unless absolutely necessary) is encouraged.

The audit committee should elect a chair, or acknowledge the chair if the chair has been appointed by the governing board. The arrangements for the taking of minutes of the audit committee meetings, meeting locations, and so on should be made or confirmed.

Selection or Reappointment of the Independent Auditor

The audit committee members should select or reappoint the independent auditor. Many of the details of that go into this process are included in Chapter 7. In many cases, the independent auditor is engaged under a multiyear contract, so the decision-making aspect of this may be somewhat automatic. However, even for auditors engaged under multiyear contracts, the audit committee should consider and confirm whether the independent auditor lived up to the terms of the contract in the previous year and address any problems before continuing with the same independent auditor.

If the independent auditor from the prior year will not be reappointed, the audit committee will need to begin the process of accepting proposals from independent auditors and, ultimately, making a selection of a new auditor.

As part of the independent auditor selection process, the audit committee should confirm that the new independent auditor under consideration complies with the required independence requirements. If the independent auditor is a carry-over from the prior year, the audit committee should confirm that the audit firm continues to comply with the applicable independence requirements.

Conflicts of Interests and Audit Committee Member Independence

If audit committee members are required to complete conflicts-of-interest statements, this requirement should be addressed during the planning meeting. In addition, if any audit committee member has had a change in personal circumstances or was involved in any transactions that might be an impairment to his or her independence to the not-for-profit organization, this matter should be noted so that it can be properly addressed.

Initial Identification of Accounting or Auditing Concerns

The audit committee members should be encouraged at the organizational meeting to discuss any specific or general concerns they may have regarding the not-for-profit organization's accounting and financial reporting practices, as well as any potential audit issues. These matters can then be communicated to management and the independent auditor, so that they can be addressed at future meetings, as well as in the audit plan that the independent auditor will develop.

REVIEWING THE AUDIT PLAN WITH THE INDEPENDENT AUDITOR

The independent auditor should inform the audit committee that the objective in developing an audit plan is, ultimately, to be positioned to render an opinion as to whether the not-for-profit organization's financial statements are free from material misstatement. To achieve this objective, the independent auditor develops a plan that he or she intends to use to meet this objective.

It is important that the independent auditor share the key elements of this plan with the audit committee so that its member can be confident that the independent auditor has developed a reasonable audit plan. This is also an opportunity for the audit committee members to express to the independent auditor any general or specific concerns that they have, so that the auditor, if appropriate, has time to address these concerns within the audit plan.

The ideal time for the meeting to discuss the audit plan is concurrent with the time frame during which the independent auditor is undertaking the planning phase of the audit. In case any issues arise concerning a procedure that must be performed at the end of the fiscal year (such as the auditor observing the organization's physical count of inventories), the audit scope meeting should be held prior to the end of the fiscal year.

The nature of the discussion of the audit scope meeting will generally vary with the size of the not-for-profit organization. Planning the audit of a large, multi-location organization will, naturally, involve more decisions and considerations than in planning the audit of smaller, single-location organization. The discussion here attempts to be as inclusive as possible, meaning that some of these considerations or questions may not apply to planning the audit scope of smaller organizations. That said, the following topics are appropriate to include in the discussion between the audit committee and the independent auditor as to the independent auditor's audit scope planning. If the independent auditor's presentation to the audit committee does not cover one of these topics, and which is relevant to the particular not-for-profit organization, this list will serve as a good source of questions that audit committee members can pose to the independent auditor. Note that it is not necessary for audit committee members to ask all of these questions; rather, they are designed to provoke thought and initiate conversation, so that audit committee members are better able to critically question and, ultimately, understand the audit plan.

The questions listed here will help to generate a healthy, frank discussion about the audit scope between the independent auditor and the audit committee members.

Multilocation Organizations

- At which locations will the independent auditor perform audit procedures?

- How was this selection made? Did management provide any input as to the location selection at which to perform audit procedures?
- If branch operations (or local chapters) exist, will branch visits be performed? If so, has a rotation schedule been established for branch visits so that every branch will be visited at least every x number of year?
- What is the financial reporting risk exposure for financial or other information maintained at branch or chapter locations?

Related Organizations

- Are any separate legal entities reported as part of the financial statements of the "parent" not-for-profit organization? Are these separate legal entities audited by the not-for-profit organization's independent auditor or by a different independent auditor?
- If there are different auditors, does the not-for-profit organization's auditor audit enough of the "total" financial statements to qualify as the primary auditor under the auditing standards?
- Do these organizations have separate governing boards and/or audit committees?

Transaction Cycles

- Which primary transaction cycles (for example, revenue cycle, expenditure cycle, payroll cycle, etc.) have been identified by the independent auditor?
- Will audit procedures for each of these cycles be performed every year, or will an audit rotation plan be used?

Internal Controls

- Does the independent auditor plan to assess control risk at below the maximum level (i.e., plan to test internal controls and then rely on those controls to reduce other audit tests of financial statement accounts and balances)?
- If control risk is planned to be assessed at the maximum level (i.e., internal controls will not be tested), how did the independent auditor reach this conclusion? Was it based on audit efficiency, or does the auditor believe that the not-for-profit organization's internal controls over financial reporting are not designed or operating effectively?
- Will the independent auditor test the not-for-profit organization's internal controls over compliance with laws and regulations?
- Will the independent auditor update the status of any management letter comments that were reported to the organization as a result of the prior-year audit?

Materiality

- What is the quantifiable level of materiality that will be used by the independent auditor in developing the scope of audit tests? How was this amount determined?

- Has the level of materiality changed from that used in the prior year? If so, what precipitated the change?

Fraud Risk Factors

- At this point in the audit, has the independent auditor identified any fraud risk factors that are present at the not-for-profit organization? Are these risk factors the same or different from those identified in the prior-year audit?
- How will these risk factors be addressed during the course of the audit?

Internal Audit

- Does the independent auditor intend to rely on any of the work of the internal audit function to reduce the amount of test work that the independent auditor would otherwise perform?
- If the independent auditor will not rely on any of the internal audit function's work, why not? Is the scope of the internal audit work incompatible with that of the independent auditor? Has the independent auditor come to the conclusion that the internal audit function performs ineffectively, or has found other problems with it?

Performance of the Audit

- Has the independent auditor assigned staff and management to the audit? Are these individuals returning from the prior year or has there been staff turnover?
- Has the organization been appropriately responsive in providing office space and facilities, administrative assistance, and so on to the satisfaction of the independent auditor?
- Does the not-for-profit organization provide an appropriate level of assistance to the auditor in terms of preparing schedules, supplying supporting documentation, and so on? Could the not-for-profit organization provide additional assistance to reduce the cost of the audit?
- What is the anticipated audit fee for the year, and how does this compare to the prior year? How many hours are expected to be spent in performing the audit, and how does this compare with the prior year?
- Does the independent auditor believe that his or her reporting deadlines are reasonable? Are any problems foreseen in meeting these deadlines and that would impact any regulatory filings required of the not-for-profit organization?
- Have there been any changes to accounting principles or auditing standards that will impact the performance of the audit?
- Are any other changes planned in how the audit will be performed as compared to prior years?
- Has management imposed, or suggested, any restrictions on the scope of the planned audit?

Information Technology

- Will an information technology audit specialist be part of the audit team?
- Will any computer-assisted audit techniques be used in performing the audit?
- Has the introduction of electronic sign-offs and approvals affected the auditing procedures and audit documentation requirements?
- Will security of the information systems be considered as part of the audit of the financial statements?

Other Required Reports

- Is the not-for-profit organization subject to the Single Audit requirement as a recipient of federal awards? If so, will the independent auditor perform a Single Audit and issue the required reports on a timely basis?
- Are there state charities bureaus or other regulatory agencies that will require a report from the independent auditor? Is the independent auditor prepared to meet these reporting requirements?

These questions form the basis of a general discussion between the independent auditor and the audit committee regarding the scope of the audit. In addition audit committee members should be prepared to address any other topics pertinent to their particular organization. The primary purpose of this meeting is to ensure the audit committee members that the audit scope planned by the independent auditor is reasonable, and that there is no limitation to the scope of the audit or procedures that need to be performed.

REVIEWING THE AUDIT RESULTS AND DRAFT FINANCIAL STATEMENTS

The second meeting of great importance to the audit committee of a not-for-profit organization is held following the conclusion of the audit, just prior to the release of the audited financial statements. Some audit committees review final, audited statements at this meeting, while others believe that reviewing a draft is more appropriate. As an integral part of the control environment of a not-for-profit organization, it is generally more appropriate for the audit committee to review a final draft of the financial statements before they are issued. Typically, an audit committee will not recommend specific changes to the draft financial statements, but enabling this capability should the need arise is an important precaution to take. Further, because the audit committee has responsibilities in the financial reporting process, it would seem that these responsibilities would be bypassed if the financial statements were finalized prior to review by the audit committee.

This meeting consists of two components: First, the audit committee members review and approve the draft financial statements that are presented to them; second, the audit committee members listen to the results of the audit presented by the independent auditor. By listening to these results and then asking appropriate questions of the auditor, the audit committee is better prepared to fulfill their responsibilities as part of the financial reporting process of the not-for-profit organization. Accordingly here in this section, a list of topics that might be discussed at this meeting is given, separated into those related to a review of the financial statements and a review of the results of the audit.

Review of Financial Statements

Every not-for-profit organization's financial statements are different, so it's difficult, probably impossible, to compile a list of questions that is on target and complete for each of them. Therefore, the lists to follow are grouped according to some very *general* types of questions that audit committee members might consider asking. And though these questions have been skewed toward not-for-profit organization issues, keep in mind that important specifics related to a particular not-for-profit organization might not be covered here because of the limitations just described. Also keep in mind that the primary respondent to questions regarding the draft financial statements should be management, as they have the responsibility for preparing the financial statements.

Statement of Financial Position

- Did the not-for-profit organization have adequate cash balances during the year to pay its bills and other obligations, such as payroll, on a timely basis?

- Did the cash balances exceed FDIC insurance limits during the year; and, if so, how has management addressed any perceived risk?

- Does the not-for-profit organization have an investment policy that defines the types of investments permitted to be made? Did the organization comply with this policy at the end of the fiscal year and at all times during the fiscal year? How is compliance with the investment policy monitored and controlled?

- Are all appropriate investments recorded at their fair value?

- Have all unconditional promises to give been recorded as contributions receivable and recognized as contribution revenue?

- Are any of the recorded contributions receivable outstanding for more than a few months? Are any outstanding for more than a year? Are they considered to be collectible? Are the balances from several large donors or from many smaller donors?

- How does the not-for-profit organization determine whether specific contributions are unrestricted, temporarily restricted, or permanently restricted? How is the satisfaction of temporary restrictions monitored so that appropriate amounts are transferred to unrestricted net assets?

- Has an allowance for uncollectible pledges been established? Is it based on specific accounts that may be uncollectible or is it a percentage of the receivable balance?

- Have any conditional pledges of contributions not been recorded as a contribution receivable? Is it likely that the conditions will be met and that these amounts will be recorded in future periods?

- Did the not-for-profit organization consider whether the value of any of its long-term assets were impaired during the year? Were any impairment losses recorded during the year?

- How would the physical condition of the organization's fixed assets be rated? Will major repairs, maintenance, or replacement of fixed assets be required in the short-term future?

- Has the not-for-profit organization paid vendors' invoices on a timely basis during the year?

- How are accrued expenses at the end of the year identified and recorded? What controls exist to make sure that all necessary accruals are recorded?

- Has the not-for-profit organization paid its obligations under long-term debt agreements on a timely basis? Has it complied with all of the debt covenants to which it is subject, both at the end of the fiscal year and throughout the fiscal year? How is debt covenant compliance monitored and controlled?

- Is the not-for-profit organization a party to any derivative financial instruments, such as interest rate swaps? What is the approval process before such agreement can be entered into?

- Are there any liabilities that require the significant use of estimates, such as vacation and sick leave liability or potential liabilities resulting from litigation? Have these estimates been made using similar methodologies to prior years? Does the organization have a process in place to determine whether estimates made in prior periods were reasonable when compared with actual results?

Statement of Activities

- Have revenues and expenses been reported on a gross basis (i.e., not netted against each other)?

- Did the organization's revenues increase or decrease from the prior year? What caused the fluctuation and what is the trend for the future?

- What is the process for segregating program expenses from general and administrative expenses? Are any administrative types of expenses (such as a portion of officers' salaries) allocated to and reported as program expenses? Are there supporting records and calculations to justify these allocations, such as employee timesheets?

- What are the controls used to ensure the proper recording of expenses as program, general and administrative, and fund-raising? Were any significant reclassifications of recorded amounts required at the end of the fiscal year as part of closing the books? If so, was the tracking and control system evaluated to prevent this problem from reoccurring in the future?

- How are costs for joint activities (such as those that are part program activities and part fund-raising activities) allocated?

- Do employee compensation costs include only officer compensation amounts that were authorized or approved by the governing board?

- Are costs for defined benefit pension plans and other postemployment benefits actuarially determined? Has the not-for-profit organization contributed the actuarially determined amounts? Are other postemployment benefits funded on a pay-as-you go basis?

- Were the not-for-profit organization's revenues and expenses in line with the organization's budget for the fiscal year? Provide an explanation for any significant variations from the budgeted amounts.

- Do amounts expended over the budget require specific approval? If so, were such approvals obtained? If no, what controls are in place to ensure that spending doesn't exceed the budget without the organization management's knowledge?

- Did the not-for-profit organization receive any revenues from unrelated business activities? If so, were proper computations for any resulting income tax liability performed and recorded?

- Did the organization comply with all other tax and regulatory matters, including collection and remission of sales tax, payroll taxes, disability and unemployment insurance premiums, and so on?

- Were any disallowances of expenses charged to any cost-reimbursable grant agreements? Was the not-for-profit organization required to make restitution to the grantor for these disallowances? Has adequate provision been made in the financial statements for disallowances?

Statement of Cash Flows

- Do the operations of the not-for-profit organization result in adequate cash flows to fund operations?

- Does the not-for-profit organization anticipate any significant changes in its cash flow patterns in the future?

Notes to the Financial Statements

- Has any information been included in the notes to the financial statements as a result of new accounting standards?

- Were the notes to the financial statements drafted by the independent auditor or by the management/accounting staff of the not-for-profit organization?

- Were any note disclosures from past years omitted in the current year?

Review of Audit Results

As mentioned at the beginning of this section, the audit committee engages not only in a review of the draft financial statements, but also in a discussion of the results of the audit with the independent auditor. Chapter 7 described a list of communications that the independent auditor is required, by generally accepted auditing principles (GAAP), to provide to the audit committee at the conclusion of his or her audit. These required communications often provide the framework for the audit committee's review of the results of the audit with the independent auditor.

However, the audit committee should be aware that these communication requirements are the *minimum* the auditor has to present. Therefore, audit committees should avail themselves, to the fullest extent possible, of information that the independent auditor can provide to them. To do so will likely necessitate some inquiries and probing on the part of the audit committee members, which can result in a more fruitful, in-depth discussion of these matters. To help in this regard, audit committee members may want to consider the following topics as appropriate to raise with the independent auditor regarding the results of his or her audit. These questions may serve as a means of launching these discussions.

Changes from Audit Plan

- Were any changes to the planned audit approach presented to the audit committee at the commencement of the audit?

- Were any accounting or auditing issues addressed that were not anticipated in the audit plan?

- If tests of internal controls were performed, was the anticipated outcome achieved—that is, was the auditor able to rely on these controls (assess control risk at below the maximum level) and reduce the testing of financial statements amounts and balances that otherwise would have been performed? If not, what other audit procedures were performed?

- Were there any significant delays in receiving information from the not-for-profit organization?

- Was the audit completed within the anticipated time frame? Was the number of audit hours estimated in the audit plan on target?

Access to Requested Information

- Did management provide all of the information requested by the independent auditor?

- Did management restrict in any way the scope of the work or types of procedures that the independent auditor intended to perform?

- Did management request the independent auditor to look into any particular audit areas that were not previously discussed with the audit committee? If so, what was the result of these additional procedures?

- Does the independent auditor believe that management and staff of the not-for-profit organization answered inquiries truthfully and forthrightly, without excessive probing?

- Did management approach the independent auditor with any accounting or financial reporting problems they had encountered, without waiting for the independent auditor to discover them?

Financial Statement Preparation

- To what extent does management rely on the independent auditor to draft the financial statements? Does management have the ability to prepare a complete set of financial statements without any assistance from the independent auditor?

- Does the independent auditor believe that the accounting staff of the organization is competent and well trained? Were supporting schedules and other documentation requested by the independent auditor and prepared by the accounting staff accurate?
- How many adjusting and reclassification accounting entries did the independent present to the not-for-profit organization and were recorded in the financial statements? What was the total dollar impact of these adjustments on total assets, total revenues, and so on.
- Was the number and amount of adjusting and reclassification accounting entries similar to those of the prior year? If the same or more, why hasn't management taken responsibility to record these entries on their own?
- For accounting entries proposed by the independent auditor and that management refused to record, why did management refuse to record them? Did they disagree with them in concept? Did the proposed accounting entries involve an estimate for which management believed theirs was just as good as that of the independent auditor? Did management think that the accounting entries were too small to bother with?
- Did the independent auditor insist on any additional disclosures to be provided in the notes to the financial statements and that management was reluctant to include?

REVIEWING THE INDEPENDENT AUDITOR'S MANAGEMENT LETTER AND ADDRESSING INTERNAL CONTROL ISSUES

The audit committee has a key interest in the internal control of the not-for-profit organization. An important outcome of an independent audit of financial statements is the management letter (sometimes referred to as the letter of representations), which contains the independent auditor's suggestions of improvements to be made to the internal control or operations of the organization. Accordingly, it is important for the audit committee to spend time discussing the not-for-profit organization's internal control with the independent auditor.

The audit committee reviews the management letter and discusses internal control with the not-for-profit organization for a number of reasons. Internal controls clearly have an impact on the organization's financial reporting, so the audit committee has an interest in them. The audit committee is responsible for the relationship with the independent auditor, and two of the benefits to be gained from the independent audit of the financial statements are comments and recommendations on internal control. In addition, the audit committee itself is part of the control environment of the not-for-profit organization. In that respect, the audit committee has a role in following up on management's responses to the management letter comments, to make sure, one, that the important issues are being addressed and, two, that management regards responding to and acting upon the recommendations seriously.

As described in the chapter on internal control, findings reported in the management letter can be classified as material weaknesses in internal control (extremely serious and rare), reportable conditions (serious and required to be reported by the independent auditor to the audit committee) and other recommendations (may be somewhat serious or may simply be recommendations for improvements in operations or for cost-saving or revenue-enhancing measures.)

To be sure, the audit committee's responsibilities as to internal control go beyond reading the management letter; nevertheless, it makes sense to review the management letter and have a discussion about internal control at the same meeting. The management letter may be a focal point of this discussion, but the audit committee members should expand their questioning about internal control to go beyond what is reported in the letter. To that end, the following discussion questions may serve to open a productive exchange between the independent auditor and the audit committee regarding internal control. At the same time, because it is management that has direct responsibility for designing and operating an effective system of internal control, they should participate in this discussion as well, rather than just responding to the independent auditor's management letter comments.

The audit committee's use of the internal audit function to assist it in fulfilling its responsibilities regarding internal control was also discussed in a previous chapter of this book on internal control. As part of its efforts to fulfill these responsibilities, the audit committee might also seek the independent auditor's evaluation of the not-for-profit organization's internal control function. Accordingly, this section also includes some questions that the audit committee may wish to ask of the independent auditor regarding the internal audit function.

Internal Control Considerations

• Did the auditor discover any weaknesses in internal control that are considered material weaknesses or reportable conditions? Are any general management letter comments close to rising to the level of a reportable condition? Are any of the reportable conditions close to rising to the level of a material weakness in internal control?

• Does the independent auditor believe that the not-for-profit organization's internal controls improved, deteriorated, or stayed the same as the prior year?

• How would the independent auditor assess the overall control environment of the not-for-profit organization?

• Has the management letter been increasing in length from year to year, or is management resolving problems at least as fast as the independent auditor is finding them?

• Are internal control problems encountered related more to the design of the internal control, or are properly designed controls simply not being followed by the organization's staff when operating the control?

• Does management have an action plan to which it has devoted sufficient resources to address internal control deficiencies noted by the independent auditor?

- Are completion dates and responsible parties identified in management's responses to the independent auditor's management letter comments?
- Are internal controls in place to monitor the not-for-profit organization's compliance with laws and regulations, in addition to internal controls over financial reporting?
- Are internal controls in place to monitor the not-for-profit organization's revenue and expenditures, to ensure adherence to the organization's budget?
- Has disciplinary action ever been taken against an employee for a serious violation of internal control procedures?
- Are the not-for-profit organization's policies and procedures regarding accounting, internal control, and other matters properly documented and widely distributed to employees?
- How would the independent auditor evaluate the conditions of internal control at the not-for-profit organization against a peer group with which the independent auditor has experience?

Evaluation of Internal Audit Function

- Is the internal audit function an effective part of the organization's internal controls?
- Are there any ways in which the internal audit function could be improved?
- Is the internal audit function adequately separated from management, so that the scope of its activities is not influenced by management?
- Are adequate resources committed by the organization to the internal audit function?
- Are internal audit staff sufficiently experienced and trained to enable them to perform their function effectively?
- Does the internal audit function perform a thoughtful, comprehensive risk assessment of the organization when designing its audit plan for the coming year?
- Is the internal audit function flexible enough to respond to particular unanticipated internal control or accounting issues that may arise during the year?
- Have the findings of all internal audit reports been shared with the audit committee?

Hopefully, the preceding questions will not only provide audit committee members with topics to cover with management and the internal auditor, but will also give them an idea of the breadth of information to consider when fulfilling their responsibilities regarding internal control.

HOLDING EXECUTIVE SESSIONS

Effective audit committees are likely to make full use of executive sessions, held by the audit committee with one particular individual or firm, such as the independent audit firm, for the purpose of providing an environment where individuals can be more comfortable expressing their honest views and responses to questions. For example, assume the independent auditor is asked about the competency of management with regard to accounting matters. The response may be more candid when management is not present in the room, particularly if the answer is negative. Note: To maintain this "safe" type of environment, minutes to executive sessions are generally not taken.

Historically, an executive session involving an audit committee would typically involve the audit committee meeting with the independent auditor, with no member of management or other individuals present. (Discussions with the internal auditor were covered extensively in Chapter 7.) That said, the audit committee should also consider holding executive sessions with individual members of management, to include the following:

- Chief financial officer
- Controller
- Director of financial reporting
- Chief executive officer
- Chief audit executive (individual in charge of the internal audit function)
- Chief information officer
- General counsel

These members of management are those recommended by the AICPA Audit Committee Toolkit, which also recommends that executive sessions be a regular part of the audit committee's agenda for each meeting, including executive sessions at each meeting with the independent auditor and the chief audit executive. (Note that as this book was going to press, the AICPA was in the process of preparing specialized toolkits for not-for-profit organizations and governments. The following discussion is based on the general AICPA toolkit, because the specialized versions were not available in time for inclusion. For those interested, the toolkits are, or will be, available on the AICPA's website, www.aicpa.org.) Meetings with the individuals holding the other positions listed would also be regularly scheduled, but less frequently, perhaps annually. For example, the audit committee should not expect the director of financial reporting to raise his or her hand at an audit committee meeting, exclaiming, "I need an executive session with the audit committee!" This is not likely to happen unless there is some major problem. However, if the director of financial reporting is scheduled for an executive session with the audit committee in advance, that individual is far more likely to be of assistance to the audit committee in terms of hearing his or her opinions and advice on the organization's internal control and financial reporting matters.

Although small and midsized not-for-profit organizations will likely not have individuals in all of the positions listed (for example, the roles of the chief financial officer, controller, and director of financial reporting may be performed by the same person) that should not alter the fact that audit committees of not-for-profit organizations should hold executive sessions with the appropriate members of management within that organization. In addition, the audit committee of a not-for-profit organization should also consider meeting with two other individuals:

- Director of development/fund-raising
- Grant compliance officer

The AICPA Audit Committee Toolkit also provides an excellent listing of questions appropriate for executive sessions with each of the individuals listed. These questions are designed to promote conversation and dialogue between the audit committee and the individual; they are not intended to serve as a checklist. And though these questions are primarily focused on publicly traded, for-profit organizations, in the following sections you'll find questions from the AICPA Audit Committee Toolkit that are tailored for not-for-profit organizations.

Chief Financial Officer

- Did the chief financial officer (CFO) sign the written representation letter provided to the independent auditors? Were there any matters in the letter that the CFO was at all uncomfortable with providing such representation?
- Do you believe that the independent auditors conducted an appropriate audit of the financial statements?
- Are you aware of any instances where accounting was used to manipulate the reported amounts in the financial statements?
- Are you aware of the occurrence of any type of fraud within the organization?
- Do you think any of the not-for-profit organization's accounting treatments are overly aggressive or too conservative?
- Does the organization perform any activities that provide any threat to its tax-exempt status?
- Do you think the organization just barely complies with laws, regulations, or grant agreements, or is a better effort put forward to surpass minimum compliance requirements?
- Does the organization participate in any activities with which you are uncomfortable?
- Are you aware of any accounting, compliance, or other matters that are being violated by the other members of executive management?
- Are there other questions that were not asked by the audit committee that should have been asked?

In addition to the questions posed to the CFO, the following additional questions might be asked of the controller:

Controller and Director of Financial Reporting

- Are there any changes to the financial statements that you would make if you were the CFO of the not-for-profit organization?

- Are you aware of any disagreements between management and the independent auditors?

- Are you aware of any disagreements between management and the internal auditors?

- Do you feel comfortable raising issues without fear of retaliation?

Chief Executive Officer

- Did the chief executive officer (CEO) sign the written representation letter provided to the independent auditors? Were there any matters in the letter that the CEO was at all uncomfortable with providing such representation?

- Do you believe that the independent auditors conducted an appropriate audit of the financial statements?

- Are you aware of any instances where accounting was used to manipulate the reported amounts in the financial statements?

- Are you aware of the occurrence of any type of fraud within the organization?

- Does the organization perform any activities that provide any threat to its tax-exempt status?

- Do you think the organization just barely complies with laws, regulations, or grant agreements, or is a better effort put forward to surpass minimum compliance requirements?

- Does the organization participate in any activities with which you are uncomfortable?

- Are you aware of any disagreements between management and the independent auditors?

- Are you aware of any disagreements between management and the internal auditors?

- Are there other questions that were not asked by the audit committee that should have been asked?

Chief Audit Executive (in Charge of the Internal Audit Function)

- Does management cooperate with the internal audit function?

- Do you have adequate resources to effectively fulfill your mission? Is management cooperative in providing these resources to the internal audit function?

- Does management view audit findings in a positive way (i.e., as opportunities to improve the internal controls or operations of the organization) or does management view findings in a negative way (i.e., they are defensive about findings because they may point to areas where management may have been lacking)?

- Has the appropriate "tone at the top" been set by management with regard to the importance of and the compliance with the internal controls of the organization, particularly those involving financial reporting?

- Are you aware of the occurrence of any type of fraud within the organization?
- Do you think any of the not-for-profit organization's accounting treatments are overly aggressive or too conservative?
- Does the organization perform any activities that provide any threat to its tax-exempt status?
- Do you think the organization just barely complies with laws, regulations, or grant agreements, or is a better effort put forward to surpass minimum compliance requirements?
- Do you have the freedom to conduct audits as necessary throughout the company?
- Were you restricted or denied access to any information that you requested?
- Did management ever pressure you to change findings or soften the language used to report a finding so as not to reflect poorly on another member of management?
- Are findings and recommendations given the appropriate level of discussion needed in order to satisfy the issues that were raised?
- Do you feel comfortable raising issues without fear of retaliation?

Chief Information Officer (CIO)

- Does the organization participate in any activities with which you are uncomfortable?
- Do you feel comfortable raising issues without fear of retaliation?
- Are safeguards in place to ensure that internal controls that involve electronic approvals of accounting entries or disbursements are adequate?
- Does the information technology function have adequate resources to fulfill its function?
- Describe the overall approach to ensuring the security of the information stored electronically by the not-for-profit organization. On a scale of 1 to 10 (with 10 being the most secure) how would you rate the organization's security over electronic information?

General Counsel

- Are you satisfied that the not-for-profit organization complies with its federal and state financial reporting obligations?
- Are you aware of any issues that could cause embarrassment to the organization?
- Have you ever been told anything in confidence or otherwise that would embarrass the organization if it were known publicly?
- Have you discussed any matters with the CEO, CFO, or others, including outside counsel, that the audit committee is not already aware of?
- Are you aware of any disagreements between management and the independent auditors?

- Are you comfortable raising issues without fear of retaliation?
- Are you aware of any activities at the executive level of management that you consider a violation of law or regulation?
- Do you think the organization just barely complies with laws, regulations, or grant agreements, or is a better effort put forward to surpass minimum compliance requirements?
- Does the organization perform any activities that provide any threat to its tax-exempt status?
- Does the organization participate in any activities with which you are uncomfortable?

Director of Development/Fund-Raising

- Has management ever requested that you not record unconditional promises to give received from donors in the accounting period in which the promise was made?
- Has management ever requested that you not record a restriction on a contribution received from a donor that was, in fact, temporarily or permanently restricted?
- Have you participated in identifying any program activities that also include a fund-raising appeal? Has the issue of allocating the joint costs between the two functions been discussed with you?
- Has management ever requested that you provide incomplete or misleading information to a potential donor to improve the organization's chances of receiving the donation?
- Have you provided the financial personnel within the organization information about obligations that the not-for-profit organization might have undertaken as part of split interest agreements entered into with donors, such as charitable gift annuities?
- Does the not-for-profit organization comply with the Internal Revenue Service regarding reporting information to donors, such as the meal cost of fund-raising dinners, providing written acknowledgments for contributions over a certain level, and so on?
- Does the organization perform any activities that provide any threat to its tax-exempt status?
- Does the organization participate in any activities with which you are uncomfortable?

Grants Compliance Officer

- Do you think the organization just barely complies with laws, regulations, or grant agreements, or is a better effort put forward to surpass minimum compliance requirements?
- Does management set the appropriate "tone at the top" that compliance with grants is an important area for the organization?

- Are employees who consciously violate grant agreements appropriately reprimanded or disciplined?
- Describe the internal controls that are in place to enforce and monitor compliance with grants. Do you believe that these internal controls are adequate? What improvements would you like to see made to these grant compliance controls?
- Did any grantor notify the organization of a violation of a grant agreement? Was the not-for-profit organization required to return any grant funds to the grantor because of the violation?
- Has the organization lost any annually renewed grants because of noncompliance with grant provisions during previous periods?
- Are financial reports required to be prepared for grantors? Is the financial information in these reports consistent with that contained in the not-for-profit organization's accounting system? Are these reports adequately reviewed for accuracy before being released to the grantor?
- For cost reimbursable grants, how does the organization accumulate direct costs to charge to the grants? How are indirect costs charged? Is there an indirect cost allocation plan that allocates indirect costs consistently to the organization's grants and programs?
- Are there any current disputes with grantors regarding grant compliance? Is there any exposure that the not-for-profit organization will have to return funds to these grantors?
- Does the organization perform any activities that provide any threat to its tax-exempt status?
- Does the organization participate in any activities with which you are uncomfortable?
- Is the recipient a direct or pass-through recipient of any federal awards programs? If so, are these programs sufficiently large to require the not-for-profit organization to comply with the Single Audit requirements? Were these requirements met?
- For federal awards programs, how has the not-for-profit organization ensured that the costs charged directly and indirectly to those programs comply with the appropriate federal requirements, as published in grant circulars by the federal Office of Management and Budget?
- Has a copy of the Single Audit reports and the organization's corrective action plan been provided to the audit committee? If not, why not?

SUMMARY

The purpose of this chapter is to provide audit committee members with the tools necessary to implement the best practices described throughout this book. This chapter offers a hands-on plan to guide audit committee members in the appropriate direction so that they may hold effective audit committee meetings. To that end, numerous questions have been provided to assist audit committee members in generating meaningful discussions with management, the independent auditors, and others. Often, audit committee members may not be familiar enough with certain areas or topics to feel comfortable in formulating and asking good questions of these other parties. Therefore, having these questions in hand when preparing for an audit committee meeting will enable them to fully participate in each and every audit committee meeting.

Index